A Special Friend

Brian Netley

Published by New Generation Publishing in 2012

Copyright © Brian Netley 2012

First Edition

www.newgeneration-publishing.com

New Generation Publishing

This book is dedicated to Andrew and Christopher and to all Ebet's relations and friends.

FOREWORD

After Ebet died, friends and family members told me various stories about their experiences with her, which were quite new to me. I realised there was even more to Ebet than I thought.

It was as if I had been living beside her for nearly 50 years, whereas others had seen/known her 'face to face'. What a revelation!

This led me to the idea of producing a book/biography/memoir about Ebet's life.

I contacted a literary friend, who knew Ebet through being a reader of the 'Parish News' for the blind and partially sighted, to try to find someone who could help. Ann is a member of a Writers' Circle and she approached another member, Sheelagh, whom she knew had written a biography.

Following a meeting with Sheelagh, she agreed to take on the task.

From there, we agreed an outline plan, which included asking family members, colleagues and friends if they would like to take part by submitting 'pieces' relating to their friendships with Ebet.

I hope you find this book enjoyable and worthwhile.

Many, many thanks to Sheelagh for all her hard work and helpful advice.

'IN THE SWEETNESS OF FRIENDSHIP
LET THERE BE LAUGHTER
AND THE SHARING OF PLEASURES'
(Kahlil Gibran 1883 - 1931)

Elizabeth Netley, known variously to friends and family as Ebet or Liz, was very gifted. Trained as a teacher, she had a lasting influence over many students throughout her years of teaching.

As well as drama, her other skills included painting, carving, sculpture, knitting, cookery, gardening, needlework and embroidery. She loved to create original projects and many friends remember her wonderful 'Alphabet Book', which she illustrated with paintings of different animals.

Liz had a deep love of nature and, for some years, kept a 'nature diary' in which she noted her observations of birds, plants and flowers in words and drawings or paintings. She loved music, reading and writing, and often produced entertaining accounts of humorous incidents in her everyday life. She also wrote poetry and drew cartoons.

She was lively, energetic, articulate, creative and deeply interested in all aspects of life. As a faithful wife and devoted mother, she cared for her family, nurturing her sons, and passing on to them her love of wildlife and botany.

She was a member of Holy Trinity Church in Bradford on Avon. Here, she was one of a small group of people who made monthly recordings of the church magazine for the visually impaired, as well as submitting articles to the magazine herself.

Above all else, Liz was a friend.

Many people consider themselves fortunate to have one real friend during the course of their lives. Liz had a countless number. And friendship to her was not superficial or simply a matter of friendly acquaintance. She loved her many friends deeply, making time for them all, keeping in contact and remaining close to each, however far away they might be.

She had that rare gift of empathy, so that she knew exactly how to respond, whatever the situation. Indeed, several friendships began because Liz found someone in need and responded with kindness, generosity and practical help.

Liz was full of fun and humour and the times together recalled by her friends, are frequently those of laughter.

Her gifts were thoughtful, individual and frequently home-made especially for the person concerned; many of these being treasured for life.

Friends covered the whole age range. She had a wonderful ability to relate with young people, especially her students, and kept in touch with a number of them, long after they left school and moved away.

Not having had an easy relationship with her own mother, she acquired a succession of other 'Mothers' during the course of her life, and kept in touch with each of them as long as they lived. These included Brian's mother, known as 'Mum Netley', Jenny de Garis's mother, 'Mum Wells';

'Mum Prudom', Helen Taylor's mother, 'Mum Woodcock', who was Issy Harradine's mother, and Julia Archer's mother, 'Mum O'Brien'.

Parents

Liz's father, Godfrey, was Scottish. His father was an Episcopalian minister, as were his Grandfather and Uncle. Godfrey's father died when Godfrey was very young and his uncle helped to bring him up.

The background of Liz's mother, Betty, remains a mystery. Betty herself always refused to speak about it. After her death, members of the family were able to do a little research which concluded that she may have been a Russian Jewish refugee.

Mandi O'Neill, Liz's daughter-in-law contributes the following:

"Godfrey had married Ebet's mother, Elizabeth Beatrice Bowden – or Betty, as she was known - in February 1938 in Port Said, Egypt and it seems they set up home in either Jaffa or Jerusalem.

Much of Betty's early life is shrouded in mystery but we have started to piece together some of her history. One clue we found after she died was a dictionary in which she had written, 'Betty Bowden, Jaffa, 22/10/36' (followed later by 'Betty Simmins, 2/2/38' - the day of her marriage to Godfrey). A search through the various databases on the Israeli Genealogical Society's website revealed that a Batia Cohen, a Palestinian, resident in Jerusalem, had changed her name to Betty Bowden in April 1933. Searching further back, we found a Batia Cohen, aged 2, listed in the 1922 census for Petah Tikva and Tel Aviv, as living with her parents Yaakov, 38 and Sara, 37 and sisters Zehava,12 and Rivka, 5, in Neve Shalom, which was an area inhabited mainly by Russian Jews who arrived in Palestine during the Second Aliyah. A burial record on the JewishGen website shows a Yaakov Feibush Cohen, born in Gomel, Russia (now Belarus) in 1884, died in Tel Aviv on 30 December 1930.

It is difficult to say for certain at this stage that this is Betty's family but it is clear that at some point there was a change in Betty's life because, as she told Ebet (and it was also noted on her marriage certificate), she had an adoptive father, a Londoner by the name of Alexander Bowden, who was born around 1891.

This change in Betty's life is perhaps reflected in some of the photos from her albums that Ebet kept after Betty's death. Some show her in a garden in Jerusalem in 1931 – 'my garden' as she writes - and others show her enjoying trips to Egypt in 1934 and other tourist sights in Palestine, looking very glamorous and clearly enjoying a comfortable lifestyle. Others show her dressing up in various guises, a hint of the love of the theatrical which she passed to her daughter. However, Betty also told Ebet that Alexander Bowden died in 1935 in a motorbike accident and subsequently his family had arrived and thrown her out of his house. A report in the Palestine Post, dated 16 April 1935 and a later obituary dated 21 April 1935, records the funeral of a Mr A

J Bowden, who died from injuries sustained in a motorcycle accident. He was buried in the Protestant Cemetery, Mt Zion, Jerusalem. Records show that he was married in England in 1912 and had a daughter, Gertrude, in 1914.

Perhaps it was his wife and daughter who evicted Betty because by late 1936 she was living in Jaffa.

Between late 1936 and early 1938 we are not sure what Betty was doing but at the time of her marriage in February 1938 she was noted as a Typist in Abu Sueir which was a British RAF base in Egypt.

Hopefully, the Israeli Genealogical Society will be able to help with further research and shed more light on Betty's earlier life."

Liz's Early Life

Elizabeth Simmins was born on 26th June 1942 in Jerusalem. Her father was the chief veterinary officer for Palestine, as part of the Colonial Service. When Liz was about four years old her mother took her to Scotland, together with her brother Bill, some three years older than her, where she was put into the charge of her Great Aunt, where she remained for about five years; Bill was placed in a boarding school.

In about 1947, the trustee-ship of Palestine came to an end and Liz's parents returned to the UK. In 1952, her father obtained veterinary work in Surrey and the family moved there.

WINIFRED COOK
Written by Brian

Winifred knew the Simmins family in Palestine and was Ebet's godmother. Her marriage was for a very few years, due to the death of her husband; there were no children. Ebet and I did not know Mr Cook.

When Ebet and I were courting, Winifred was living and working in Surrey, so we saw her occasionally. She did, of course, attend our wedding.

When she retired, Winifred moved to the New Forest and later into sheltered accommodation at Barton on Sea. We visited her on several occasions, taking her into the forest and such like for outings. She visited us on a number of occasions, including one memorable Christmas, when I had problems collecting her in heavy snow.

When she died, I attended her funeral on behalf of Ebet, who was unable to attend due to work commitments.

Names
Liz was christened Elizabeth.

However, when she was very young, her effort at saying her name came through as 'Ebet'. Consequently, that became the name by which she was usually known, except when she was naughty when her mother would say 'ELIZABETH!'

Her best friends, and of course her family, knew her as Ebet. Other friends during her younger years knew her as Liz or Lizzie. At college, the only name she gave to new friends was Ebet.

When she returned to teaching in Wiltshire, she used the name Liz, because it was easier. There was then a tendency to use Liz more generally.

We have decided, while producing this book, for the most part to use 'Liz', but have not sought to impose that name for contributions from those who knew her otherwise.

Teenage years

Now living in Surrey, Liz attended a local girls' convent school and joined the local church youth group where she first met Brian. The two of them were instrumental in starting a Bible-study group with other members of the youth club.

At the age of 17, Liz left the convent and attended the local technical college where she gained the qualifications she required to get a place at Whitelands Teacher Training College in Putney, to study to become a teacher, her special subjects being English and Drama.

She made lasting friends at college and they relate many stories of college exploits. She had already developed a keen interest in drama and this was reflected in various 'skits' she produced while at Whitelands. Those who were there with her will never forget, amongst others, 'Washing the Elephant'.

During her final year, in addition to college work, final exams, writing to Brian and various drama projects, Liz took over the job of college social secretary.

Romance

Brian, meantime, had been enlisted for National Service and had been posted to Singapore and then Malaya. While he was there, he and Liz exchanged occasional letters, although there was no hint of romance at that time.

However, when Brian was demobbed in 1960, they met once more at church and Brian invited Liz to go on a date. They went to the pictures and saw 'High Society'. This date was to be the beginning of a relationship which lasted for over 50 years.

Waiting until Liz was in her final year of training, they announced their engagement in February 1963.

Soon after term ended at Whitelands, the two were married in August 1963. They had a home because Brian already owned a new bungalow, but had let it for a year or so before the wedding. This came as a great surprise to Liz's parents, who knew nothing about it until the engagement was announced.

Early married life

Liz obtained a post teaching English and PE in a comprehensive school in Camberley and then taught for a short time at a local primary school, before starting her family.

In 1966, Liz gave birth to Andrew and two years later Christopher was born. In 1970, Brian obtained a job as an accountant in Warminster and the young family bought a house in Bradford on Avon where they remained for the rest of their married life.

While the boys were growing up, Liz stayed at home to care for them, keeping her hand in with some occasional supply teaching. Although not working full time, Liz was never idle. Besides caring for her children, she spent much time gardening, cooking and in creative projects such as drawing, painting, tapestry and sculpture.

Back to school

In 1983, she took up a post as a drama teacher at George Ward School in Melksham, where she remained for five years. She passed her driving test during this time so that Brian no longer needed to drive her to school each day.

She then moved to Lavington School, near Devizes, where she taught drama for seven years before moving to Clarendon school where she worked part time until her retirement two years later, in 1997.

Liz was no conventional teacher. Her lessons were unusual, great fun and her students adored her, as did many of her colleagues. She was a fierce champion of the students and was able to spot the potential in those who had been written off as 'trouble makers'. She produced some spectacular shows which past students still remember, giving many of them a love for acting that has lasted throughout their lives.

Retirement

Brian had retired in 1996, due to ill health, and the two of them made the most of their opportunity to spend time together. They bought a motor-home and went off on many short breaks, as well as longer journeys to Ireland and Scotland. Leaving the motor-home behind, they made trips as far away as the USA and Australia. There were regular reunions with two of Liz's old college friends and their husbands.

In between these trips, Liz remained busy with a variety of creative 'projects'. She spent much time in making personal gifts for her friends, many of which are treasured to this day.

Her expertise as a drama teacher was called upon, even after her retirement, and she was invited to run an in-service training course for teachers at Urchfont Manor.

Celebrations were an important part of Liz's life. She loved to plan and prepare for these and many will remember both the silver wedding celebrations and the ruby wedding weekend, details of which appear later in this book.

In 2008, Liz became ill with what was to be her final illness. She spent time in both Bristol and Warminster hospitals, where many friends visited her. She faced her illness and her coming death with the same courage and sense of humour as she had faced the rest of her life, typically worrying about how her family would cope without her.

Liz died in Warminster on January 2nd 2011. Her death left a large hole in a great many lives.

Her funeral was attended by a huge number of people, each of whom had his or her own story to tell of a special relationship with Liz. There were so many stories and so many memories that it seemed fitting to gather them together into a book to be shared by all who knew and loved Elizabeth Netley.

***

"IN-LAWS, OUT-LAWS AND OTHERS'
The Family

Family was important to Liz. She was a wonderful mother to her own two boys and she also embraced the other young people in the wider family, mainly her nieces. They were all welcomed into her home and she faithfully kept in touch with them all, by letter and telephone calls.

It wasn't just the younger members of the family who benefited from her care; she was always ready to help anyone of any age, and cared for Brian's father when he became ill.

Liz's own mother was never an easy person and she and Liz were never close. However, she moved to Bradford on Avon in 1977. After she retired, Liz saw her mother regularly, taking her on many trips in the car (Betty having had to give up driving). When she could no longer manage on her own, Betty had much help from carers, Liz not being strong enough to manage on her own, but doing as much as she could, until Betty died in 2006.

Her artistic instinct was how she viewed the world
ANDREW NETLEY
Son

My mum was known for her many interests and most involved a love of art and nature. It was her passion in these areas that had a huge impact on my life, and enriched it enormously. Although I didn't perhaps always appreciate the extent of her influence when I was younger, much of the encouragement I received in childhood has come full circle – both in my work and the way I live today.

Whilst growing up with my brother, my mum put huge effort into organising things for us to do, both in the holidays and after school. Most of these, as you would expect, had an artistic bent, and aside from painting and drawing we tried just about every medium of art materials on everything from t- shirts to eggs. We also made costumes and models and - my favourite at the time - collages. As we grew up and my mum returned to teaching, her enthusiasm and encouragement were passed on to many of the kids she taught.

Her other great interest that was to have a lasting impact on me, was her love and knowledge of nature, particularly wild flowers and birds. I remember her saying that she couldn't decide which she liked most. She was forever getting us to learn and identify wildflowers. Despite her repeated attempts to get me to distinguish sheepsbit scabious and rosebay willowherb, I never managed it, but the names are indelibly imprinted on my memory. However, she did succeed with birds and I'm constantly surprised how easily and quickly I can identify the birds I see and hear today.

In the last weeks of my mum's life it was difficult, sometimes, for her to express herself verbally but we spent time together looking through images of textiles and birds and she was still inspired enough to try and sketch out her ideas. Her artistic instinct was how she viewed the world and I feel very lucky to have shared that with her and to have some of that gift passed on to me.

She taught me the difference between knowing the path and walking the path
CHRISTOPHER NETLEY
Son

I saw my loving and lovely Mum not only as a selfless, endlessly patient and inspiring teacher – but also as a timeless and beautifully trained student of ornithology, botany, literature, the performing arts, sculpture, science and nature, natural history, paintings, etchings, classical music, reading, writing, cookery….knitting and logic puzzles!

As my teacher, she taught me the difference between knowing the path and walking the path. As a fellow student I considered myself very fortunate to have inherited and to have shared many of her interests. However, my attempts to follow her lessons were not always as successful.

Two of my more challenging subjects were botany and ornithology. The former could have so easily earned me an F minus! Whether we were walking amongst the horse chestnuts, elms and oaks, the green fields of Wiltshire or even in Bradford on Avon she was always well prepared with a selection of reference books, binoculars and a flower press. In those early days anything beyond dandelions, daisies, stinging nettles, sheepsbit scabious and rosebay willowherb, was almost as difficult to fathom as their Latin translations.

However Mum truly had the patience of a saint and I knew she wasn't going to let me get away with it so easily! Perhaps with a combination of intuitive foresight and careful planning, Mum and Dad often invited me to look after their garden whilst they were away for some well earned time together. As they inevitably took the much needed rain with them on holiday I had a challenging time keeping their thirsty flowers maintained, but also took the opportunity to teach myself a few of the finer points of botany and enjoy the variety of colours and perfumes - everything from the sweet peas, roses and azaleas to the glorious poppies, sunflowers and delicately expressive orchids. It was definitely 'thyme' well spent!

Thanks in part to the programmes and narrations of David Attenborough, my classes in ornithology went somewhat more smoothly and I swiftly (no pun intended) progressed from the ABC of cute, fluffy yellow ducklings, teenage cygnets and moorhens (or coots as I could never tell the difference) to the XYZ of the colourful plumage of winged teal, pink flamingos, the water dance of the great-crested grebe and the waltz of the birds of paradise.

Our field trips to Rode Bird Gardens, Stourhead, and Slimbridge brought my lessons off the pages of illustrations and television and into the sunshine of reality. Watching them in their own world, listening to the diversity of their songs or feeding them within arm's length, made me appreciate what Mum had been so patiently teaching me for so long.

I'm not sure if I ever managed to pass my exams but I think I know the path a little better and walk it every day with the confidence she inspired in me, and the endless love of her soul.

It must have been great to have had her as a teacher
BRENDA SIMMINS
Sister-in-Law

I met Ebet in 1970 at the time that I met her brother Bill, who was to become my husband.

Ebet and Brian lived at Yately at the time and we went to a party there. She was very easy to get on with, lively, funny and a lovely person.

Brian and Ebet then moved to Wiltshire and so we didn't get to see them more than a couple of times a year, when we also visited Bill and Ebet's mother who lived there, too.

I loved their house. It was full of books of all sorts and interesting ornaments. Ebet was a great collector and a very knowledgeable person. It must have been great to have had her for a teacher.

Ebet always came up with fun things to do for Andy, Chris and our children when we all met up. She also gave very interesting, thoughtful and creative presents.

Ebet was such a fun and happy person and even when she became ill she was still very cheerful during our phone calls, laughing and covering up the fact that she was in pain.

I wish we had seen more of Ebet and I do miss our telephone chats.

Aunty Ebet was fun, fun, fun!
TANYA WHITE and LARISSA HARDEN
Nieces

Larissa

Aunty Ebet was fun, fun, fun. That's how we remember her, always full of smiles, laughter and making others laugh.

When we were very young and used to visit Aunty Ebet, Uncle Brian, Andy and Chris in Wiltshire, we always had such fun. We used to play in their garage dressing up and exploring their wonderful house with all of the beautiful and unusual knick-knacks.

We always remember and looked forward to any birthday and Christmas presents from Ebet as they were always so different, creative and fun. We both used to say how we would have loved for Aunty Ebet to be our teacher as we are sure that she was a wonderful teacher who made learning fun.

Whenever we visited our Nanny (Ebet's mother) in Wiltshire, we always looked forward to Aunty Ebet coming over to see us. She lightened, brightened and filled the room with happiness and laughter.

We always remember Aunty Ebet and Uncle Brian going on holiday to wonderful places.

Tanya

Aunty Ebet was my godmother and in 2008 I had my twin girls and from then on we used to speak or write to each other more. I always loved getting her cards and they always made me laugh, she had such a good and amusing way with words.

She was always thoughtful with all of our children. We just both wish that she had met my daughters Sophie and Emily and Larissa's daughter Isobel. Ebet had only met Alexander, Larissa's son.

Aunty Ebet was such an amazing lady during her illness; when I used to speak with her she was full of laughter and humour, so much so that you would never think she was so ill. She was an inspiration and a wonderful woman and I miss our catch-up chats.

Aunty Ebet will always remain our fun and happy Aunty in our memories and thoughts.

Being feisty, she held her own
ROSEMARY HUTCHINS
Sister-in-law

Elizabeth was a wonderful kind, warm, talented, clever and extremely vibrant person, so full of amazing ideas and invariably well able to achieve whatever she put her mind to.

I met her when she was about 12 (and I was 15/16) as she began to come to our Young Communicants Guild, where her brother Bill was already a member. As a Church group we spent many hours at meetings, outings, walking, cinema and, of course, church. Bill was a very good friend and the group was always thriving - it shaped the teenage years of quite a number of young people; some came quite a way to join us. When Elizabeth joined she was 'the little sister' but, being feisty, she held her own and made sure she had her say.

In about 1957, a new group called the Aspasians was formed, made up of the 'older' members and the Dramatic Society, which was also connected with the church. My brother, Brian, had been one of the leading proponents for this new group, but left in late 1958 for National Service. I recall that, on his return from Malaya, Brian and Elizabeth started their friendship, which flourished, leading to their marriage in 1963 and continuing until Elizabeth's premature death in January 2011.

When our daughter, Alison, was born in November 1963, we asked Elizabeth to be her godmother, which she willingly accepted. When Christopher was born in 1968, Elizabeth and Brian asked me to be his godmother, which was very special to me.

Elizabeth and Brian lived near us in the early years of our marriages (Keith and I had married in 1960, when Brian was still in Malaya), so we saw a good deal of each other, but when they left for pastures new in Wiltshire in 1970, it was only three or four times a year that we got together, but those times were very memorable indeed!

When our father, Edwin (known mostly as Ted) had a heart attack, followed by extreme depression, in the early 1970's, it was darling Elizabeth offered to have him to stay for, I believe, at least 5 to 6 weeks, during which time she cared, bullied, argued, ranted and cajoled him back to good health. It was an incredible feat considering the boys were very young and needed plenty of attention (not sure how much Brian received during that time). Anyway, <u>defeat</u> was never an option for her and she won the day and our 'Dad' was well again.

No doubt other friends and family have mentioned Elizabeth's ability to argue and talk 'the hind leg off a donkey' when in the mood, and it was best not to have a high opinion about anything unless you had time to debate and really knew your subject!

Elizabeth was cruelly taken from us far too soon but she leaves behind such a legacy for us all. Her tenacity and determination to fight her illnesses, all through her life, with such fun and fortitude is truly a lesson to us all.

A wicked sense of humour
ALISON WEBB
Niece and god-daughter

My Auntie Liz was a wonderful lady with a strong character and a wicked sense of humour. She was very special to me as she was my godmother.

The connection is: Rosemary is my mum and she is Brian's youngest sister, which makes Liz my auntie through marriage.

She was chosen as my godmother, and as such, we always had a special bond.

Although we did not live close to each other as I was growing up, we did meet up at all the regular Netley family gatherings, of which there were many over the years, although sadly Liz's health did prevent her from attending some of the functions.

But she did attend my christening, my confirmation and my wedding. I still have my picture bible that she gave me on my confirmation.

Auntie Liz and I kept in close contact while I was in my late teens and over the years, keeping in touch by letter; both she and I really enjoyed writing and she gave me lots of good advice and her wonderful positive attitude to life always made everything seem OK.

I was devastated to hear of her awful illness and we all kept hoping the doctors would find a solution, but sadly not. Living in New Zealand and not able to come home easily, meant that I was unable to see her before she died, having last seen her eight and a half years ago, when we left the UK.

We did, however, correspond by mail and it was incredible that, although she was the one who was suffering, she still wrote to me with positiveness and also sent me a beautiful gift of a silver chain with a bright red heart and I will treasure it forever.

I did return in June 2011, to attend my brother's wedding, and met up with Uncle Brian and Cousin Chris for a lovely family reunion, although someone very special was missing from the occasion.

Uncle Brian had wanted mum and I to choose a few pieces of Liz's jewellery while we were visiting, so I now have a few more reminders of her.

The house was just the same; full of owls, ornaments, pictures and masks and I particularly loved the cushions she had made, all showing what a talented, interesting lady she was.

My other biggest memory is how Liz took care of my granddad, Ted Netley, when he was suffering from depression. I also had a very special relationship with him as my granddad (having bought me my pony when I was 10). I recall how Liz spent time and care with Granddad and made him well again.

During my visit to Uncle Brian's during my recent trip to UK, we went over to the cemetery so that I could see where my lovely Auntie Liz has been laid to rest. I was very emotional but I think I needed to see where she was to actually believe it. It is a beautiful place but she shouldn't be there yet, life just isn't fair.

I was amazed at her strength and determination
ROBIN NETLEY and BARBARA WARNER
Brother-in-law and sister-in-law

One of my earliest memories of Elizabeth concerns a Brains Trust in the church hall at Addlestone where, later, her wedding reception was to be held.

I was friendly with her when she was in her early teens taking instruction for confirmation. At the time she was probably 13 years old and a pupil at St Anne's Convent, Chertsey. Strangely, one of the panel was 'Jock' Brady, my headmaster at Strodes Grammar School, Egham, who was a very strict disciplinarian and a formidable Oxford history and legal academic.

During the debates Elizabeth stood up and, to my horror, challenged 'Jock' on one of his statements. As usual, he tried to silence her with one of his condescending put- downs, but Liz was made of sterner stuff. Basically she outsmarted him and eventually he gave in with a stupid grin. I was staggered by this show of intellectual strength and it was the only time I had seen 'Jock' humbled.

Elizabeth was also physically tough. I recall an occasion about the same period when I needed help to transport my kayak to the canal in New Haw, a distance of more than a mile. It required one person at either end with wheels under the centre, in order to trundle along the road and avoid any traffic. To my surprise, Liz offered to assist and, once again, I was amazed at her strength and determination.

Robin's sister, **Barbara**, adds: I was at that Brains Trust, sitting next to Robin. I looked over my shoulder and saw this feisty young girl, aged about 13, and whispered to Robin, "Who is that?" to which he replied, "Bill's sister."

How we loved her and oh, how we miss our feisty, delightful, talented, loving sister, Liz!

A very cheerful person with a strong personality
PETER NETLEY
Brother-in-law

My first definite recollection of meeting Liz was at St Paul's Secondary School, Addlestone during 1960, when I was twelve years old.

I did have a vague memory that I had seen her previously; probably she may have visited our house since she knew my brothers and sisters through the various church activities and clubs. I do remember that she was always a very cheerful person with a strong personality.

That first meeting that springs to mind was during a science lesson .Liz had either started at Teacher Training College or was considering it as a career, and in order to gain some experience of running a class, had agreed to come along to St Paul's. I seem to recall that she was introduced to the class by our usual teacher shortly after the

28

lesson had started, who then retreated to a safe distance!

We were being instructed in the art of glass making and I was making a pipette (or a test tube, I can't quite remember after 52 years). Either way it involved heating glass tubes over a bunsen burner (I don't recall that we wore any protective gear, Health and Safety didn't seem to get in the way in those days).

Anyway, Liz was obviously in charge of the class, and happened to come over to see what I was doing, possibly because she recognised me.

"I'm making a pipette Miss" I said.

"Oh right "she replied, may I have a look please (or words to that effect).

Of course" I said, handing it over.

She always maintained that I burnt her hand deliberately, but nothing was further from my mind. However, the incident was often brought up whenever we met, as her first introduction to her 'horrid' little brother-in-law.

Another occasion was during 'The Winter of '63', I believe it was February.

I was living with my parents in Mytchett. Brian was also living there, although he didn't spend much time at home, between working and seeing Liz, who was still living at her parents' home in Addlestone.

I recall that there had been very heavy snowfall and as it was the weekend, Brian was due to drive to Addlestone to visit Liz who didn't drive.

I can't remember if I badgered him to let me go with him, or whether he offered to take his 'kid brother' (unlikely!). Any way we set off. He had an MG Midget sports car and as I remember, it was a bit of an adventure as we weren't sure whether we would make it.

We left Mytchett and went via Deepcut. There weren't many other idiots on the road, especially in low slung cars. When we got to The Maultway, which was a very straight road in open country from Deepcut towards Bagshot, we encountered snow that seemed to be two feet deep (things always seem bigger when you're young!) and due to the minimal ground clearance of the Midget, it seemed likely that we would have to return home.

Just as we were about to attempt to turn back, a vehicle appeared which resembled a car from the 'Waltons'. It was straight out of the 1930's, very upright with wheels about three foot in diameter and two inches wide, driven by a couple from a similar era. It seemed to be able to move effortlessly through the deep snow, and we were able to follow its tracks, until we reached Bagshot where the roads were clearer.

When we reached Addlestone, Liz was surprised to see to see me accompany Brian. I don't remember that we stayed too long as we obviously needed to get back before conditions worsened.

Needless to say, we made it home unscathed.

Liz used me as the subject for a Child Study during her training whilst at Whitelands College.

However, I was not aware of this study until many years later (probably twenty years ago) when she threatened to expose this tome if I was stroppy with her. As far as I know, no one else apart from, possibly, Brian has ever seen it.

She gave it to me to keep a few years ago and it is in a safe place. It is interesting to read her views of me, and the relationship with my parents and siblings, and one day I will hand it on to my children.

My overriding impression of Liz was that she had a very generous personality; she always seemed to give more than she took. She is sadly missed.

Think pink on a black day
JO NETLEY
Niece and god-daughter

'Think Pink on a Black Day' is the title of a poem given to me by Auntie Liz, something I've treasured and endeavoured to live by and for which I am thankful to her. It's fair to say she embodied that motto. Colourful, kind, imaginative, intelligent and never dull. Her fabulous personality and presence brought love, laughter, warmth and joy to any situation. She gave a lot to others and left this world a better place for it. An example and an inspiration. That's how I remember my godmother Auntie Liz.

Nothing was too much trouble
JULIA SHORTER
Sister-in-law

I was one of the 'outlaws' - in other words Liz and I married a 'Netley'. Liz and I always laughed at being an 'outlaw'! There were five 'outlaws' - Roy, Keith, Liz, Patricia and myself. When we were all together there was always much hilarity and fun - happy days!

I remember when we used to stay with Liz and Brian, she was always a joy to be around and the 'hostess with the mostest'.

When preparing a meal, her kitchen looked as if a bomb had hit it, but they were always yummy meals. When younger I was always envious of her culinary expertise and her totally relaxed manner in the kitchen, as I was nervous of entertaining the 'Netleys' because there were so many of them. I'm not like that now though, thank goodness!

Very often, Liz made our Christmas presents - painted and varnished stones, papier maché birds or mobiles, etc - everything individual, and the time and effort she put into it was amazing.

My memories of Liz are those of a very caring, welcoming person; nothing was too much trouble. Her caring was shown to Dad Netley when he went to stay with her to convalesce after a serious illness. She was the only one who could get him back, and she had to be 'bossy' and even managed to get him to paint a picture by numbers!

Liz was a star and he came home from Liz much better than when he went.

SHARING LIFE ON WALPOLE STREET

Liz attended Whitelands College from 1960 until 1963, where she studied English and Drama. A typical student, she worked hard and played hard as well, making the most of her time and often staying up most of the night in order to meet essay deadlines. Many of the friends she met at college remained friends for the rest of her life, even those who moved to the other side of the world.

Liz already knew Brian when she started college and he was a regular visitor; although in those days there were strict rules about guests and they had to leave the premises by 10pm. Their relationship survived this regime, however, and they secretly planned to marry as soon as possible after Liz finished college in 1963.

This shorter, more rounded and dimple-smiling extrovert
JENNY deGARIS

Ebet was one of the first fellow-students I met when I started at Whitelands College in Putney, southwest London in September, 1960. Tall, a bit over-solemn and fairly introverted, I was intrigued by this shorter, more rounded and dimple-smiling extrovert. We were both allocated rooms on Walpole Street – one of the residential corridors of our Anglican teachers' college named after streets in Chelsea where the college had originated. Since our group of students were the first to be studying

33

for three rather than two years, we were to have plenty of time to establish life-long friendships.

Except for this seemingly random room-allocation I might not have been among what became the longest-lasting of friendship groups that included Ebet, since our study and practice timetables had little overlap. She took English as her main subject whilst I opted for Divinity. She was training to become a secondary teacher, whereas I was aiming at upper primary. And in our second year she was elected as one of the student 'reps' who attended College Council and sat for meals at High Table. However, we had laughed together enough during first year to later agree to share one of the rare flats – Ebet inhabiting the inner room, while I had the outside one. This meant we used my room (as the most accessible as well as the larger of the two and the one with a gas fire) as our social space, and it was in part there that the links were forged between the four of us, Ebet, two other secondary-teaching students, Helen and Issy (Helen Taylor, née Prudom, and Isobel Harradine, née Woodcock) and me. Together we smoked and gave up smoking; planned parties, excursions and plays for the college stage; discussed everything from religious and political issues to families, boy-friends, books, college gossip and essays to be written – sometimes also with mutual friends from other groups. Living in close proximity meant that Ebet and I also shared – if sometimes involuntarily – in each other's last-minute efforts at completing assignments. The tendency to live to the full by day and write during the night was a trait we had in common.

Ebet had to go through my room to get to hers, but gained the privacy she needed in her developing relationship with Brian: they could enjoy precious time together when he came up from Surrey at weekends. The college rules were strict in those days. Men were only permitted in student rooms for limited hours.

For going out ourselves in the evenings or over the weekends we were obliged to sign a book giving details of our whereabouts and times of leaving and returning to college. The chief person in charge of this system was our Deputy Principal, Miss Phillips. This job, together with her being generally inflexible in her demands of high standards, encouraged the rebel in me, together with a couple of others, to cook up a prank. We rang an order for a large barrel of beer to be delivered to her room 'for having a party with my students' (!) At the point when its recipient returned the beer and required the perpetrators to own up and apologise, Ebet – always one to encourage positive outcomes in human relations – felt we should step forward. This was a time she and I were in disagreement. I felt that our deputy principal could have afforded to turn the joke back on us by receiving the beer with better grace and actually throwing a party! (Ebet's ethical stance prevailed though: I did finally go and own up to the phone call!)

Ebet's attitude undoubtedly resulted in part from her sympathetic nature, which was always ready to defend the sufferer. For herself she rarely complained, or if she did it was humorously in the third person, as in her occasional wry announcement, 'Unfair to an Ebet!'

Ebet left college in 1963 to marry Brian and live in Surrey. Helen and I shared flats and taught in the East End of London for the eighteen months until I married Brian de Garis – a West Australian Rhodes Scholar who was doing his History PhD in Oxford and whom I'd met at a Student Christian Movement Conference in Bristol during our last year at Whitelands. We then came to live in his home city of Perth.

Ebet wrote regularly to me and for 45 years selected and sent a beautiful Christmas card each year to me and Brian. This was often accompanied by a thoughtfully chosen gift, sometimes hand-made by herself: an embroidered bookmark; a miniature book, such as the exquisite '*snow*', by Maxence Fermine or my last gift from Ebet, the 2010 Christmas package of a pair of miniature *Wooden Books: ISLAMIC DESIGN* and *SACRED NUMBER*. At various stages Ebet also gave me jewellery. I still have a lovely enamelled bead necklace she gave me at college, and when, a couple of years ago, I sadly reported to her the theft of another necklace she'd given me – a substantial jet-bead one of her mother's – she immediately posted off the smaller jet one she had kept for herself. And perched on my current study windowsill is the perfect little Irish Leprechaun Ebet left me as a thank-you for their visit to us in 2001 when we were spending two years at

University College in Dublin, reminding me that life is precious, but we mustn't be too precious in response to it!

Leaving my mother country – landscapes, seasons, family and friends – was more difficult than I had begun to imagine. Sympathetically, Ebet 'adopted' my mother, calling her 'Mummy Wells'. She kept in touch too, with my sister, Fiona, the youngest of my three siblings. Being the oldest I'd taken on for my littlest sister something of a mothering role and she was only 13 when I left England permanently to go to the other side of the world. When our mother died in 2005 I found among her treasured keepsakes a lovely letter from Ebet which typified my friend's thoughtfulness: in it she had written what is all too frequently not spoken to the living person – a statement of her esteem for 'our Mum' and the reasons for it.

Another continuing connection was the gift Ebet and Brian gave me in asking me to be Andy's Godmother. This is not a connection by frequent correspondence, but I remember Andy showing me his first significant art photos, and now think of him as I watch these wonderful BBC Bristol wildlife documentaries and feel proud when I see his name against the Editor heading. It's always enjoyable for me to catch up with him in person, as my Brian and I did when he and Mandi made us welcome in Llanfihangel-Tor-Y-Myndd as part of my 60th birthday celebration weekend in 2002. There we were impressed by the great job they were doing to restore their cottage. We admired their garden and met their menagerie, before driving on across to share our pleasure with Ebet and Brian. It's not every Godmother has a Godson who wins an Emmy! Nor every mother who has such a son, and I know Ebet was very proud of Andy and happy for him. I know she was also proud of Chris, whom I haven't myself known so well, but have the impression of a person of great courage and integrity – like his mum.

It was an unusual pleasure when Brian and Ebet came to spend time with us in Perth in 1986, and to share Ebet's enjoyment of Australian birds and landscapes as witnessed by her poem in our guest book.

Our return visits to England have been sporadic, but almost every time Ebet and Brian have made us welcome in their home, from when we arrived with two small daughters to the time I'd come alone to spend time with my ageing mother in Surrey. I'd managed to book into a weekend of creative writing at Urchfont Manor as my personal 'extra' for the visit. I didn't ring Ebet until I'd arrived there and discovered there would be a short interval of 'free time'. She nonetheless made a generous effort to drive over from Bradford on Avon to see me. I remember how she shared with me her delight in her new RED SPORTS CAR . . .

For the de Garis family our longest time back in England was 1976-77 when we celebrated the Queen's Silver Jubilee Year in the Sussex village of Ditchling. Several of my college friends and the husbands and children they then had joined us at our cottage in Underhill Lane for the August Bank Holiday weekend. Of course the four Netleys were among them.

My last time with Ebet was in 2009 when Brian and I were on our way between Cornwall and Wales. We were hoping to be able to catch up with the Netleys, but, knowing Ebet was undergoing the terribly draining cancer treatments we hesitated to contact her. When I finally did ring, however, our friends decided they would meet us halfway to where we then found ourselves: at my brother's place in Tetbury: So it was the Cinnamon Café in Corsham for an excellent lunch and talk together. My Brian and I were surprised when Ebet declared she wanted us to come back with them to Bradford for tea! This we did and thus caught up with recent acquisitions to her (& sometimes Brian's!) eclectic collections of glass, sculptures, pictures, plants . . .and a renewed sense of both Ebet's generosity of spirit and the wide range of her interests and circles of contact.

Having effectively said my goodbyes that day, I didn't expect to feel the need to be at her funeral. When the day was almost upon me I realized I must be there: Not quite so simple from the rural southwest of Western Australia. However I was lucky enough to find a seat on a flight leaving Perth about nine hours after I'd decided to go, and even luckier to be in it when the plane took off! I thought how Ebet would have been chuckling at my last-minute effort.

It was good to be there with college friends,

with my sister, and with Brian and Andy and Chris to find a space for both grief and delight in the memories we shared of being together with Ebet.

We shared a love of the Goons
ISOBEL HARRADINE

My earliest memories of Ebet are of our college days together at Whitelands in Putney in the early 1960s.

We shared a love of the Goons and a small group of us would gather round Ebet's tape recorder to produce our own version of the show, complete with mad sound effects. What a brilliant 'Eccles' or 'Bluebottle' she was!

I also remember her as Charlie Chaplin in a college review. Ebet bent an 'iron bar' with a great show of effort only to have it spring back instantly when she let go. It was actually a spring from a common room chair!

After leaving college most of our contact was by letter and what entertaining reading Ebet's letters were.

When Chris and Andy were very small Peter and I stayed with Ebet and Brian in Surrey. Jenny and Brian were also staying with their little girls. I was filled with admiration for the way Ebet managed to organise the household and feed us all extremely well and still be such fun to be with!

Over the years, as the children grew, our families met up for short stays with each other. Ebet always knew how to keep the children happy!

On one occasion she did a 'Sun Dance' in Norwich Cathedral Close because it was raining – sure enough the rain stopped and the sun came out!

Later, with the children grown up, we met up for twice yearly breaks with Ebet and Brian and Helen and Stewart. There was always so much laughter on these trips particularly when we went to Russia where the hilarity was not solely fuelled by vodka!

Ebet and Brian's Silver and Ruby wedding celebrations showed their great generosity in kind, but more importantly, of spirit. How lovely it was to see Ebet really revelling in being with her family and friends!

How Peter and I miss Ebet's friendship and sense of fun!

Duly delivered to the door by the local coal merchant.
HELEN TAYLOR

So many snapshots full of love and laughter flash through my mind going right back to 1960 and Walpole Street at Whiteland's College. Ebet's room was opposite mine.

The 'Chaplinesque' mime by Ebet, of washing an elephant, in the Student Review was a show stopper and so outside the experience of this farmer's daughter from North Yorkshire.

How well Ebet made the minimum of money stretch, even to entertaining Brian by preparing food for him in our basic College kitchen. We so enjoyed special events together and how she helped me to value my Mum and her food parcels - she sent me fruit cakes and roast chickens by parcel post! Such as we shared on one hilarious birthday celebration - accompanied by the cheapest of cider, much to the chagrin of a certain lecturer who demanded that I seek out the source of the disturbance and admonish the noisy perpetrators.

Ebet hitch-hiked, with Jenny, to the farm and was duly delivered to the door by the local coal merchant. That gentle warmth and appreciation made her a great hit with Mum who received cards from her for the rest of her ninety six years. Special to me is the lovely acceptance note for our wedding, kept by Mum but unseen by me until last year. I talked to Ebet about it then.

The week after our college life ended was the beginning of the biggest adventure of Ebet's life. Brian and she married. We had all seen and, to some extent, shared the blossoming of this romance over the previous three years, Brian sweeping up in his sports car and sharing life on Walpole Street. I took the National Express bus back to Surrey from the North to join the celebrations.

Over the next few years I would turn up on their doorstep with the latest boyfriend until I married Stewart and moved to Carlisle. Though living far apart we shared wonderful moments in our children's' lives and Ebet was Kerina's Godmother.

There was 'fenders and tackers' (defenders and attackers) at the Roman Fort of Birdoswald on Hadrian's Wall with this special lady bringing the battle to life.

Again, as she crouched, halfway up the staircase with our tiny children at Dalemain, a Cumbrian country house, to create a story about the Mouse family that lived in the Mouse House that had been built into the step there, how her zest for life shone out.

More recently, we have enjoyed holidays with Ebet and Brian and Issy and Peter. The sights and sounds of St Petersburg and Moscow being a particularly memorable one; sharing the sleeping compartment, drinking vodka, the interruptions by the armed guard.

We have shared many short breaks in this country, too, enjoying new places, reminiscing and simply enjoying being together.

In between and over all these years there have been the shared confidences and wholehearted, unstinting love and support via long phone calls and letters.

The best of friends who is missed so much and will never be forgotten.

Presents were never dull or predictable
KERINA LYNCH
Goddaughter

I have really good memories of "Aunty Ebet" from my childhood. Although we lived a long way away from her, I remember the letters that she would write to me that were always encouraging and interesting to read. I would reply a few weeks later and give her my updates.

She had a great way of connecting with me through her letters during all the different years of my life. So it was always a fun thing to receive them and reply; telling her about my exploits, from summer caravanning holidays with my family and the detailed reports I wrote to her concerning swimming in the sea with my friends and shouting "minnow alert" when we spotted little fishes, to long and heartfelt letters as an adult, explaining the choices I was making in my adult life, related to my Christian faith.

As a child, birthday and Christmas presents were looked forward to; as presents from Aunty Ebet and Uncle Brian were never dull or predictable.

Over time I recognised her love of literature, culture, art and crafts through the gifts she chose too. I can picture, and indeed still have, a number of the gifts that she gave me over the years (which for someone who has a tendency to clear things out regularly is quite an achievement).

Through my university years I also appreciated the letters from Ebet and it somehow linked me a little to her and my Mum (Helen Taylor) more, as they met at college and were good friends ever since. I, too, met some very good friends at university and have continued friendship with them, some twenty years later.

After university, when I travelled down to

Bradford on Avon and the surrounding area, I stayed with them and enjoyed connecting on a personal level with Ebet as an adult, without my parents being there.

We had a lovely time. I can particularly remember going to see a lovely garden at a stately home and Ebet doing cross stitch to a really high standard. This inspired me to think about being more creative and I wondered if I could do cross stitch some time.

Soon after that visit, I received a cross stitch bookmark from Ebet, which I currently use.

I got married in October 2007 to Craig Lynch. Ebet and Brian were able to come up before the wedding and Brian took some photos of me and my bridesmaids getting ready in my house, and Craig at a friends house nearby eating bacon buns. I really appreciated this as I was not keen to have the official photographer while I was getting ready. This was an echo back to my parents wedding where he took some cine film, including my mum getting ready, which they now have on video or DVD.

I am sure that Ebet is now in heaven and is fully enjoying herself there; I look forward to meeting her again.

We had many interests in common
WENDY WYLD

I remember Ebet being a fellow student on Walpole and having a boyfriend, Brian, who had a car and took her out at weekends. My friend Isobel, who was also a student at Whitelands, kept me posted about Ebet over the years. We met Ebet and Brian at the weddings of Isobel's two daughters, so Simon and I were on the edge of Ebet's life until her last illness.

During that time (about two years), Ebet and I corresponded by letter, cards, cuttings etc., and found that we had many interests in common. These included nature, especially flowers and birds, gardening, children's stories, poetry, travel history and quirky things made of silver, wood and china.

In one sentence; "Ebet and I got to know each other again through the art of letter writing and 'craft from afar'."

Brian adds: I particularly remember Wendy at Whitelands College and her boyfriend, Simon, visiting her there. On our last holiday, a cruise around Britain, we met Wendy and Simon at Oban, near their home. They were allowed on board because Ebet was too unwell to go ashore. Our friendship was sealed!

***

'A TEACHER AFFECTS ETERNITY'
(Henry Adams 1838 - 1918)

It was obvious from the start that Liz was a gifted teacher. She enjoyed her work and threw herself into teaching drama. There were regular school productions directed by Liz. These were highlights for many of her students, and for some of them it was the first step into a life of acting. For others, it gave them much needed confidence as well as tremendous enjoyment and a sense of achievement which they never forgot.

She was also a much valued member of staff and made many lasting friendships in the various schools in which she taught.

Twinkling eyes, a throaty laugh and anarchic plans
JOHN KENDALL

I joined George Ward School in 1981 as a Biology teacher, and I think Liz arrived about two years later to teach Drama and English.

Our paths crossed in the staffroom, and I have a clear picture of her twinkling eyes, a throaty laugh and anarchic plans (but always a deep commitment to the children's needs).

On occasion she exuded fury at the inanities of management or someone's appalling manners - a fearsome sight! We were both involved in the staff drama group's production of Bond's play 'The Sea'. She said later that she worried I had truly taken on the tailor's personality and was descending into madness. The thought quite appealed to her though!

By and by Liz found the restrictions of our school too claustrophobic and left for Lavington in 1988. Our lives went their separate ways.

Some twenty years later, in 2008, Michael and I were having lunch at Papillon, a little French restaurant in Bath we frequented. Pascal, the owner, produced brilliant food, and as Tamas, the Hungarian waiter (for whom Liz had a soft spot) said, "It is more like a club."

The tables were very close together and you quickly got to know other regulars, discussing the menu and anything else.

One day as we were enjoying our meal the voice of the woman next to me began to ring vague bells, and I realised there was something familiar about her. By the time pudding arrived the penny had dropped - it was Liz! I turned to Liz and said, "I know you," and Liz said, without any hesitation, "Hello John."

She and Brian were also Papillon addicts. With a shared interest in the Arts and Crafts movement our lives overlapped effortlessly once more.

Sadly our renewed friendship had all too short a run.

A forward-looking and intuitive person
MARGARET DAVIES

I first met Liz when she joined the staff at Lavington Comprehensive School as head of drama. She very quickly became a highly respected teacher, form tutor and work colleague. She was also hugely talented as a drama teacher and was very good at knowing how best to inspire and encourage her students.

Drama became a very popular subject at the school across all year groups and Liz even managed to get staff involved.

On the last afternoon of the autumn term, several of us, including members of the senior management team, presented a pantomime for the whole school. The students certainly appreciated seeing their teachers make fools of themselves. They cheered and booed in all the right places and found it all great fun. Liz's panto soon became a pre-Christmas 'must' at Lavington School.

Liz and I worked well together as teaching colleagues. A non-examination course we introduced for Years 10 and 11 was given the unusual but imaginative name, Dimensional Studies. It incorporated music, dance, drama and RE (my own subject), and was jointly led by the respective heads of department. Selected topics such as 'Listening' and 'Conflict Resolution' were explored, with students spending a couple of sessions per topic with each teacher before moving on to a different teacher and a new subject area.

As a spiritual education course, Dimensional

Studies was innovative, popular with students and, in several respects, ahead of its time.

Liz was certainly a forward-looking and intuitive person and was never slow to stand up for true justice, fair play and social inclusiveness whenever and wherever she found them wanting. I admired her energy, her wisdom and her commitment and found her to be a much valued friend and work colleague.

It was very special for me to be asked to cover the gospel reading in the service of the celebration of her life at Holy Trinity Church, Bradford on Avon, especially as I had been at her bedside and prayed for her shortly before she died.

I have many happy memories of Liz and am grateful for her enduring friendship and support over many years.

Mrs Netley made you feel like a star
LUCY GOLDING

Mrs Netley was quite simply the greatest teacher I, and many of the people lucky enough to be taught by her, have ever known.

When putting together my thoughts for this letter I have smiled, laughed and cried remembering what a profound influence my drama teacher had on my young life and how her impact is still felt in my life today.

Stepping into the drama studio at Lavington was a truly magical experience and the magician was Mrs Netley. At once we were transported to a maze with monsters waiting, a train station with sinister happenings, a village in the grip of the Black Death. Mrs Netley's imagination knew no bounds and she was generous enough to share it with all her pupils.

The school musicals and talent nights were a testament to that enormous generosity and unstoppable spirit – the cast lists rivalled Ben Hur, because our drama teacher never turned anyone away; everyone was welcome.

For that short time we were all stars in our own lifetime because that's how Mrs Netley made you feel; like a star. It's hard to put into words what that does to you as a young person and how rare it is in a teacher to make not one but all of her students feel like that. For me, it was down to Mrs Netley that I started to think that anything was possible, that I could do things that I didn't think I could. I believe this was because she was fearless, or at least seemed it to me, and so she passed that on to us. "Don't think you can sing? Well you will sing in the next school play."

"Don't think you can dance? Well you will find yourself bopping around the school hall in front of all your friends and family."

And always, alongside you, cheering you on was Mrs Netley. I close my eyes and I can see her bounding around that big hall, singing and dancing and spurring us on with her boundless energy and enthusiasm.

It was only later on that I realised the enormous work that she put in to the plays, musicals and talent nights. She was scriptwriter, director, producer, lighting, back stage, the list is endless –

she was quite simply everything – the beating heart of all school performances. How lucky we were to benefit from her huge talent and, once again, her generosity

I have so many memories of Mrs Netley: Whizzing around in her red soft top car, our last drama lesson with her – an epic adventure in the woods which resulted in us rolling her down a hill, twigs in her hair and a smile on her face – how many other teachers would happily let a bunch of 16 year olds do that?! Mrs Netley could because she knew we respected and loved her and being so free with her was an expression of that.

I remember her coming to the pub with her husband Brian to celebrate our leaving Lavington. We arranged it with Brian without her knowledge. He even took a roundabout route to get to the pub so that she didn't guess where they were going.

We wanted her there because she was one of us and we were going to miss her like we would miss a great friend, because that's what she was, a really great friend.

Mrs Netley was quite simply the best teacher I have ever known, and more than that she was one of the best people I have ever met. She had a saying that she wrote on our shirts when we left Lavington: 'May your future be all brightness'. Well Mrs Netley, my future was bright and you can take a lot of credit for that. Thank you for making me believe I could do anything, and I for one think the world is a little less bright now that you have left us - but how you lit it up while you were here!

She understood me when others didn't
BENJAMIN D JOHNS

Liz, or Mrs Netley as she was known to me, was my favourite school teacher and the best teacher ever.

She was my form teacher for years 4 and 5 and drama teacher for years 3, 4 and 5. We got on very well from the first few months of knowing each other. I was very happy when she became my form tutor. She understood me when others didn't; she knew what made me tick. We became very close. Liz was my inspiration. She encouraged me to open my creative mind; she introduced me to improvisation which I use heavily in my creative practice as a film director. She saw I had potential as an actor and young person and pushed me to develop skills. A number of teachers had written me off as a rebel without a cause.

We also had lots of fun and Liz had a wicked sense of humour. She transformed the drama department at Lavington School and was like a breath of fresh air.

We had tremendous school productions in which Liz directed me. Two of my favourites were 'The Boyfriend' where I played the dapper 'Lord Brockhurst' and then an original play written by Liz where I was 'Snick' the evil goblin with a green face and my hair back brushed so it rose a foot off my head. Naturally I kept it like that for when I went into assembly!

Liz was very supportive of me. There is one event which really encapsulated how much she would 'go the extra mile'.

I wanted to raise some money for the homeless charity, 'Shelter'. Liz suggested I write a poem which I could then perform in assembly, and make a collection. She helped me write the poem which was a moving piece written by a tramp about his thoughts and feelings, I would dress up as the tramp.

I got my costume together; an old dirty mackintosh and plastic bags on my feet. I took it to another level when I kept the left over dinner for the past week. When the day came, even Liz was surprised when I smeared the smelling food all over me!

The performance went very well. It was at lunchtime when I was going up and down the queue for lunch begging students for money that the headmaster (with whom I didn't get on) told me to stop. I did, for a couple of minutes and then carried on.

He came back a second time and the same thing happened. I was in role and I wanted some more money. The third time he came back he was very angry and started shouting and marched me to his office. The stinking food was much to his dislike.

Liz had been informed of the situation and was summoned to his office. The headmaster wanted to suspend me for the rest of the day. Liz was having none of it and told me to go and wait outside. They then had strong words where she told him that if he suspended me then she would leave too. The headmaster backed down and I had to go and wash off the food and get back in school uniform.

We collected nearly £200 for Shelter. Liz and I had wicked smiles on our faces when we gave him the money a few days later, to send to the charity.

After I left school I kept in touch with Liz and updated her on progress through 'A' levels, University and beyond. I would send her post cards from wherever I was travelling and keep in touch.

She was a massive influence on me and if it wasn't for her I wouldn't be doing what I do now. She truly was inspirational to me and to a whole generation of young people whose lives she touched.

The last time I spoke to her I told her about some problems I was having at University where I was teaching. She said, "No one treats my Ben like that – I will go down and give them what for."

She was a wonderful, caring and warm person with a fantastic, creative mind.

When I have a problem or get into a sticky situation I know she is with me helping me to find a good solution. I know she was very proud of my achievements. We were happy in the knowledge that we showed the people who doubted me that they were wrong.

Thank you Liz for being you and everything you have given me; you will always be a part of me.

Liz was fearless!
ALISTAIR PEARCE

Liz started teaching in our school during my last two years there as a pupil, some twenty three years ago. However, my memories of her are as fresh as if it were only a week or so ago.

Very much a larger than life character, I think the first thing that as a young adolescent I appreciated about this new teacher, was that she was different from all the others in the school (I too seemed to be very different from all the other pupils in our school!).

The school at that time was only a small local village church-maintained comprehensive, with no more than 500 - 600 pupils, so anyone slightly different or 'from out of town' was immediately noticed - but there was something else about this lady that got my attention and it wasn't just her slightly alternative dress sense (although that of course played its part). It was her strength of character that was so refreshing to witness, probably because I was at that age struggling like many others to understand my own. To put it bluntly, Liz was fearless!

Unfortunately, GCSE Drama wasn't introduced into the curriculum until after my 'year' had chosen our GCSE options, but I had always got heavily involved with any of the school productions and was delighted that Liz was herself so passionate about the Arts.

I remember the production of 'African Jigsaw' that Liz produced not long after her arrival at the school and I remember my appreciation at having been given a substantial part in the said production. Without a doubt, Liz planted a seed in me and that humble seed has ultimately grown to shape the course of my entire life.

I think it was sometime in the middle of my final year when Liz gathered about six of us from the year group together, saying how she wanted us to enter a young writers' competition. Her total belief in our abilities and her, by now, infamous powers of persuasion saw the six of us create a short play entitled "Heaven or Hell", in which we all starred. The basis was human morality, based around the consequences of certain life choices and, ultimately, death, where we would end up.

Anyhow, the upshot of it was that Liz must have seen something in us that we didn't - our little production went on to win in the finals and was performed by us in the Theatre Royal, Bath.

Not long after this, Liz asked what I was going to do once school had finished. I remember the pain I felt as I replied, "Oh, I'm going to work for my dad, as his apprentice".

My father was himself very much a larger than life character, a plasterer by trade and also at that time Chair of the school's governing body. Many a time I had felt the embarrassment and shame of having the whole school know this fact. At important assemblies my dad would sit next to the Principal on stage, seemingly oblivious to the pokes, punches and gibes I would be receiving, as I sat amongst my peers.

"You're going to do what?" Liz replied,. "Be a

plasterer's labourer?"

"Yes," I said, "He wants 'And Son' on the van".

"What do you want to do?" she asked.

"I've always enjoyed art and I would like to do GCSE drama at college," I answered.

I think it was the next evening at dinner my father said "I have had a call from one of your teachers today, Alistair". I remember how scared I felt. Why had a teacher contacted my father? "She has invited me in for a chat tomorrow".

"Oh," I said.

"She said it's regarding your future."

"Oh", I said again.

(We have to guess what was said during the 'interview')

The following September I attended Chippenham Technical College, where I studied a BTEC national diploma in Art, Design and Photography and also GCSE Drama. My love of the Arts has remained a constant in my life and has seen me join several amateur dramatic societies and, in later life, I returned to education, studying Performing Arts at a BTEC level and subsequently a BA Hons. degree at Bath Spa University in Dance and Drama Studies, graduating with honours in 2006.

Liz's strength of character has profoundly influenced and indeed inspired me not only to accept my own differences but also to celebrate them, enabling me to live a life that is true to me.

Having experienced working as a supportive

artist on such TV programmes as 'Casualty' and 'Being Human', I have, for now, hung up my performing hat and have taken up the rather more respectable role of 'Child Care Officer', working with young adolescents with Asperger's syndrome. My passion, it seems for now at least, is a desire to enable young people to express themselves freely and to celebrate their differences. Just as in the same way Liz did with us.

I only hope I will be able to inspire their young minds as Liz did mine.

I hope we did her vision justice
ALEX STARK

Liz Netley, or more appropriately from a student's perspective, Mrs. Netley, was not only the most extraordinary of teachers, but was possibly one of the most exceptional people I have ever had the pleasure of knowing.

I choose my superlatives carefully, especially in today's world of 'here today and gone tomorrow'. But quite simply, the time I spent under her care and tuition as a student form some of the happiest memories I have of my formative years.

As a pupil at Lavington School from 1989-1994 I can remember little time when I and my friends were not pre-occupied, either with preparing for a school play, rehearsing a sketch as part of a comedy night, or just eagerly anticipating our next drama class.

I loved drama as a student, but whilst attending

my first rehearsals for a performance at my next school after Lavington, I quickly realised that it was Mrs Netley's care, attention, commitment, and I believe love, that made her truly unique.

Never before, and never since have I had a teacher who dedicated so much enthusiasm, so much energy, so much passion, and so much expectation into her classes and her productions.

Particularly fond memories are those of performing in her productions of Peter Rose and Ann Conlon's 'African Jigsaw' and Peter Skellern's 'Trolls.'

Ably supported by Mr. (Tony) Jones on keyboards, Mr (Derek) Heather on percussion, and a host of backstage students and staff, she enabled us to experience the nerves preceding the opening of the curtains, the thrill of the performance and then the satisfaction of the audience's applause. We loved every minute of it, from the initial lunchtime auditions and rehearsals to the closing night party.

In addition to the school productions, I was fortunate to receive drama lessons throughout all of my Lavington years, up to GCSE examination.

I initially made the mistake of believing that because I enjoyed drama, I could therefore 'play' at it. Mrs Netley, with mock rage-like tones, regularly informed me that I needed to 'work' at drama instead. However, working at drama, I quickly realised, was immense fun too.

Performing in her production of 'Who's reality?' before HTV television critics at the Watershed Media Centre in Bristol, offered an opportunity to blend her original script-writing and arrangement with her students' own sketch work. The resultant performance, played out as a montage of eclectic life experiences, contained characters ranging from a disillusioned open-university television presenter to a clergyman being presented with a case of bigamy whilst conducting a Church of England marriage service!

Though I didn't realise it at the time, the metaphysical nature of this work made it a bold production to perform - I hope we did her vision justice.

Whilst performance was a key component in drama, Mrs Netley inspired what I enjoyed most - improvisation and sketch writing. Engagement in these activities formed the basis of my happiest school memories bar none. The structure of her lessons allowed us to explore and have a huge amount of fun with themes of fantasy, psychosis, espionage, domestic servitude, disaster, mystery, apocalypse, illness, grief, exploration, and man-eating monsters - to mention just a few!

Her efforts and support enabled and inspired my best friend and me to engage enthusiastically and passionately with comedy sketch writing - our efforts regularly performed with minor success at school comedy nights.

Many, many, happy hours were spent writing, re-writing, tearing-up, destroying, and, finally, mending our scripts ready to be performed to her in order to be 'approved' for inclusion in the big night. We laughed so much during this process, I can still remember the aching of my ribs subdued only by the final deadline panic!

These words do little justice to the impact that Mrs Netley had on my life, and I'm sure, many other students' and adults' lives. I am so grateful for the effort, patience, care, and generosity she offered me. Her utmost professionalism, dedication, and love for her students remain firmly in my heart, and vividly strong in my head.

Thank-you Mrs Netley........ and I really promise you, we'll have our next script ready by tomorrow lunchtime, yes I know, but please give us 'till tomorrow, it'll be finished, perfect even, well, perfect-ish, er, well we'll have a first draft ready by next Monday after school, is that okay?

The hand of friendship
ANN STARK

Some seventeen years ago I found myself in a very dark place. After more than twenty-five years of marriage I was now suddenly faced with the prospect of being on my own with no home, no job and three children all in full time education.

The outlook was bleak especially for the youngest who was sixteen at the time and in his last year of official schooling, though the assumption had always been that he would follow the example of his two older sisters and stay on at school to take his 'A' Levels and then go to university.

It was at this low point in my life that Liz, whom I had known initially as a working colleague at Lavington School and then as my son's much loved drama teacher, made a surprising and completely unexpected gesture.

One day she slipped an envelope into my hand and without any explanation walked away. Inside the envelope was a cheque for a not inconsiderable amount of money and a card which explained its presence.

My son, wrote Liz, was a boy that she perceived as having talent and it was her wish that he should be allowed to carry on in full time education to fulfil this potential. If a monetary monthly donation from her would make the difference between my son leaving school and finding a job and staying on to complete his studies then she would be pleased to help.

She went on to say that she had always tried to support youngsters in need, in whatever way she could. She apologised for not being able to offer more but said that it came with 'no strings' (apart from my promise of not telling my son or anyone else for the time being) and would continue until the situation had resolved itself. She did not wish to talk to me face to face about this offer.

To say that I was surprised would be an understatement. Although Liz and I were colleagues and we had always got along together, then as a supply teacher I did not see her that often as I worked at several schools and we had not socialised out of school either.

I went home and cried! I could hardly believe that, out of nowhere, had come an offer that would indeed make a difference and that someone cared enough for my son to make this sacrifice in their own standard of living.

Happily, more good things were to follow and I never needed to bank the cheques that now arrived by post. My son completed his 'A' Levels, and then took a year out to go to music college where he gained the necessary qualifications to become a peripatetic guitar teacher, should the need ever arise. He then went on to Manchester University where he gained his B.Sc. which he followed by three further years of study to gain his doctorate. All those years before, Liz had been right to have confidence in him.

On the day my son became a doctor I told him about how someone other than his family had offered to sponsor him all those years before and had had faith in his ability. He was overwhelmed and a phone call to Liz soon followed!

I have been very saddened to hear of Liz's death – far too young. However, I am happy and proud to be able to let you know just a little of what happened in secret all those years ago. My son and I salute her and mourn her passing.

A truly wonderful woman
SARAH JONES

I was a pupil at George Ward Comprehensive School, Melksham, where Liz taught English and Drama between 1983 and 1988.

I went on to Whitelands College, Roehampton, where I did a BSc (Hons) degree, and then went on to a PGCE at Froebel College at Roehampton, Surrey University.

Liz and husband Brian came to my wedding in 1996, and I continued to correspond with Liz.

When I was at a difficult stage in my life I received some very supportive and inspirational letters from Liz, to which I still refer.

I moved to Cornwall and now teach infants as a supply teacher, and have two children of my own.

Liz was a truly wonderful woman and I will always remember her very fondly. As I have said, she was inspirational to me.

Liz was a much valued drama teacher
ROGER DAY
(Wiltshire County Drama and Theatre Adviser 1975-1994)

Liz Netley loved drama, theatre and life. She attended every course on educational drama that I ran in Wiltshire and was always an amazing contributor. Other teachers respected her views and she could be truly creative. She played an active role in my Masters degree presentations encouraging the whole of Lavington School to become involved in the recreation of "Wayland Smith", a Wiltshire legend.

Liz was a much valued drama teacher and gave much to Wiltshire and its Arts Heritage.

Royalty
Written by Brian

In June 1989, the Princess Royal (as Patron of the 'Save the Children Fund') came to Devizes to honour the local supporters for their money-raising success for the SCF over many years. Some of the local schools, including Lavington, were asked to provide some entertainment such as dancing and drama at the Wharf. Several teachers from Lavington, including Liz, were involved, especially Peter Jordan who was the local organiser for SCF.

Liz was responsible for a piece of drama.

As part of the celebrations, Liz was amongst those introduced to the Princess. Also, she managed to have a few words with her during the taking of light refreshments.

A local journalist came to Liz, asking if she had been excited by meeting the Princess. Liz's response was "didn't the kids do well!". When further pressed by the journalist, Liz refused to agree with her, just repeating her original response. This was not Liz's 'do'; it was the schoolchildren's! And it was for the SCF!

This was typical of Liz - she always wanted the spotlight on the children.

Loss
JOHN YATES

In my morning ritual
   I shave and shower and carefully dress - as for a lover.
   Colleagues do not merit this (I do not seek **their** admiration).
   In the assembly hall the young faces ignore me - looking to the stage
   But in my fantasy I pretend they secretly care.

"It's just a job - and poorly paid for what we do", colleagues say.
   But don't they, too, walk on air when they hear?..
   "I've learnt so much from your lessons."
   "You've inspired our daughter."
   "I want to be in your class."

And is this not the root of our jealously?
   Don't we all grit our teeth when we say
   "They really love you."
   "Isn't she brilliant!"?
   Don't we all want a following like yours?

How many of us can foresee the loss?
   It will be duller, lazier, less just.
   They will be more complacent, less challenged, less loved.
   We will be unprotected, unheard, unsung.
   I will be more ignorant, isolated, introvert,

And you will be…

…a hint of cigarette smoke on an empty stage.

'HEARTS, LOVE AND FRIENDSHIP'

Most people have many acquaintances but just one or, at the most, two special lifelong friends. Liz was the exception to this rule. She had countless friends and was, herself, a true friend to a great many people

From that moment on Ebet and I were inseparable
BRIGID (Biddy) JENSEN

Ebet came into my life in August 1953 and became the sister I never had.

My family had just moved to Chertsey and I had not yet made any friends. My brother already went to a local school and had a friend called Bill. Bill had a sister the same age as me, just turned eleven. They were invited round for one of my mother's famous afternoon teas and from that moment on Ebet and I were inseparable.

We spent every Saturday afternoon together, either at her house or mine. We used to go off on our bikes and have lots of adventures. One of our favourite places, when she visited me, was a little creek which ran into the River Thames. We spent hours building rafts out of bits of branches and then trying to float them. Two dripping wet girls would appear for tea and mum would just ask us to wash our hands!

Our other favourite place was a large, derelict mansion house. It had a cellar and we used to dare each other to go down the stairs and see what was there. Ebet was always much braver than me so it was Ebet who finally went down, only to find herself up to her waist in murky water! Fortunately it was a very hot day and she dried out in the sun but her canvas shoes shrank so she had to walk home in bare feet and whiffing somewhat.

We were both avid film-goers and I think we saw every musical that the 50s produced. Even then she always rooted for the "underdog"

Our next series of adventures began when we started to have holidays at the Pioneer camps run by the South Africa General Mission, of course not 'PC' any more. Here we both became 'born again Christians' and very attached to the Billy Graham hymn book. We used to sing duets at evening prayers. Ebet had a beautiful soprano voice and I sang alto.

We attended these camps until we were nearly 17, the last two years as helpers, cooking and cleaning as well as having a jolly good time.

Of course by now we had discovered boys and it was at our last camp in the Lake District that Ebet announced she intended to marry Brian and we told everybody that they were engaged. Of course Brian was blissfully unaware of this but I knew she was right. Dear Ebet was always right!

It was soon time for us to leave our respective convents and start a career. Our plan was to become teachers and go to the same teacher training college but as we were only 17 and had a year to wait I went to art school and Ebet to 6th form college.

To cut a long story short I stayed on at art school much to Ebet's annoyance and she went on to teacher training college. She became an amazing teacher, changing many children's lives for the better and, as predicted, married Brian.

By now our paths separated but we stayed in touch mainly by letter. It was in our later years that I started to spend more time with her and my "bestest" friend also became my mentor.

I have never met anyone else with such generosity of spirit. You could tell her anything but she was never shocked and never judged and always had a way of looking at things and coming up with totally unpredictable answers.

Staying with her and Brian was a joy. In the mornings I sat on her bed and we became those two little girls again, arguing "black was white and yellow was no colour at all."

Ebet was a very special person and anybody who knew her would say totally unique. Unique because this wonderful, caring person suffered with very bad health nearly all her life but did it stop her? No, she was there for everybody.

Her marriage to Brian gave her the stability, love and support which she never had as a child and, with his patience, understanding and, above all, love, she was able to fulfil her potential and become the person we will never forget.

At least I married those two!
JOHN ATKINS
Written by Brian

John was the vicar at St Paul's, Addlestone, Surrey from about 1956. He knew my family quite well, there being plenty of us. He clearly knew Ebet quite well, by the time I returned from National Service. He did not see much of us while Ebet was at Teacher Training College, except during school holidays. We did once help run a 'house party' for the young members of St Paul's, knowing many of them from earlier years.

John gave Ebet and I some very helpful advice, when we attended our pre-wedding chat. He, of course, conducted the wedding beautifully, except he gave us the service booklet for funerals, so we had a little problem with getting the right prayers. We had a good laugh about it later.

Although we set up home some fifteen miles from Addlestone, we kept in touch with all our friends, including John and his wife Addie, at St. Paul's.

At some stage, John was appointed to the benefice of Walton on the Hill. When the time came for retirement, John, like most retiring priests, had to move to where he could afford to buy a house. That happened to be in Warminster, just 12 miles from Bradford on Avon, to where we had moved in 1970. So we got to see more of John and Addie.

They attended the boys' confirmation in 1986 and our Silver Wedding celebration in 1988. John made a lovely remark at the latter, "If I haven't done anything else of note, at least I married those two". What a lovely man!

Addie died in 1992 and in due course John moved to the Isle of Wight, where his daughter and her husband lived, he being the vicar at Bembridge. We continued to correspond until John died, following which we attended his memorial service at Walton on the Hill.

Ebet was always so welcoming
MARGARET EBSWORTH

I cannot remember the exact year I met Ebet. I know it was at a party at the home of a mutual friend. I cannot remember who this was but Brian thinks may have been a member of our little mission church.

I was fairly new to the company and was feeling very reserved when a friendly face chose to talk to me. It was Ebet and it was from this beginning that I found myself one day outside her bungalow with my two small children, whose ages were similar to her child.

It was about mid-morning, I can't even remember whether I had been invited, I can only presume I had as it was unlikely for me to turn up uninvited.

The scene that greeted me was wonderful; so many people I knew had homes to be seen in "House Beautiful", unlived in, not a thing out of place. Ebet's was like mine; she was sitting reading, her little boy playing on the floor around her, the floor covered in toys.

It wasn't long before my two had made themselves at home. Ebet was always so welcoming; she appeared so relaxed and we always enjoyed our visits to her home.

We were sad when she and Brian moved to Mytchett for three years, and then Bradford on Avon. We always meant to visit, although Ebet kept up with news at Christmas time.

I regret that we did not see each other more frequently and was so sorry that her life was cut short. I will always remember her.

I clearly remember nappy changing behind the settee
FIONA NASH

Ebet has always been in my life. The reality was, she seeped into my life from age eight, crept in when I wasn't looking, no fanfare of trumpets, just there and lucky for me, stayed there for my next 50 years, to then creep out – too soon!

Ebet was my sister Jennifer's college friend and so my first memory of her was when I went to stay with Jennifer at Whitelands College, where they shared a flat. I have memories of sleeping on their floor, aged eight, with all these grown up girls coming to say "hello" and making comments of "Ah…aren't they sweet?" (My other sister Mary was with me)

From this beginning Ebet took the whole Wells

family to her heart, and she to ours. When Jennifer took off for her new life in Australia, Ebet helped to fill that gap, and more…and let me say here, that it wasn't only Ebet, but lovely Brian too (buy one get t'other free, excellent value!). When they visited it was thrilling to ride out with Brian in his MG sports car (this was a family without wheels, so doubly exciting). One of my first times away from home was a ride on the train to stay with them at 'Bruins' where we stayed up extremely late playing board games and just having fun.

Regular visits from Ebet and Brian, and now their precious babies, to Chart Downs…for some reason I clearly remember nappy changing behind the settee.

Now into the turbulent teens, boyfriends were introduced, and even when one unknown turned up at their house long after I had left –all got the Netley Welcome.

Not knowing what to do with my life – Ebet was really important to me at this time and her ears were in constant use! I was a regular visitor to St Margaret's Place where I like to feel I was of some use keeping Andy and Chris occupied in return for my angst! I have happy memories of those times. One time as she, I and the boys were parting at Bradford station, both small boys burst into tears at my leaving.

Hours sitting in the moonlight outside the front door as I agonised over the decision to stay, or leave nursing – what to do….on and on I agonised, and she never showed signs of impatience with me…and then I left nursing!

I drifted on, always with her there as my confidante. The next job as a telephonist enabled me to make regular sneaky phone calls and stay in contact which was important as there was no phone at home.

By now I had met Cliff who was to become my husband - of course I had to take him for inspection – I always valued Ebet's opinion, even if I didn't always heed it!

Cliff of course was welcomed 'in' and at our wedding they played an important part, not least Brian polishing up his car to become my bridal car.

We stayed with them on our way to and from holiday, and, at other times we were just there. We were able to reciprocate their many kindnesses by having Andy and Chris stay with us for a weekend, whilst they had a break away. (Many years later, they returned the favour by having our three boys for a weekend)

Everyone's lives by now had got busy, not least mine with my three offspring, and so we didn't get to see Ebet and Brian as much as would have liked. However, we were in regular contact – she was still always there for me, at the end of the phone, full of encouragement, not least when I started to paint again.

She was one of the first to buy a painting to show that she believed in me (it now hangs proudly in Andy's loo!) And she stated that had she been well enough she would've been my agent.

It really meant a lot, when she took time out to

send flowers on the first anniversary of my mother's death. There were so many other caring little touches over the years.

I like to think I was as important in her life as she certainly was (and is) in mine. She will always feel a part of me, because I can never remember a time when she wasn't, and you never forget a person whom you love.

Fun was always the underlying theme.
IAN BACK

Soon after moving to Bradford on Avon, Janet, with her bandaged leg, saw this lady with a bandaged arm who turned out to be Ebet. She smiled and spoke.

From this conversation they discovered that Chris and our Collette would be starting the same play school shortly. From an occasional cuppa and a lively conversation, after dropping off our children at play school, our friendship grew.

Around this time, Ebet mentioned problems they were having; the kitchen table was sinking into the floor. The solution was to replace the floor, which involved Brian digging up the existing one. Janet offered my help! This was the beginning of our long friendship.

Our families started spending time together. Ebet introduced us to various games, such as Enigma, Yahtzee, as well as traditional card games. Fun was always the underlying theme.

We only lived in Bradford for two years and

when we moved to Cricklade, Janet was quite lonely. Ebet wrote each week a limerick which cheered Janet up no end.

Ebet was always seeking new experiences with arts and crafts which, in turn, through her enthusiasm, resulted in us venturing into new mediums. She was encouraging and generous about our efforts.

The things we remember her doing are: polishing stones to make jewellery, writing and illustrating, embroidery, wood carving, painting pebbles and cross stitch. We have many things she made and will constantly be a reminder of her and how she touched our lives.

Besides creating, she was also a keen collector of books, paintings, handbags and pieces of china and glass. She became quite knowledgeable about these

Both Ebet and Brian became very enthusiastic bird watchers.

Ebet's return to teaching drama was a significant part of her life, as well as in the lives of some of the young people she taught, for they remained in contact with her after leaving school.

Ebet did not enjoy good health for many of the years we knew her but it did not stop her from enjoying life and being there for others.

Slightly overdone Brussels with Sunday lunch
SPENCER BACK

1970 was, **I** think, the year we moved to Bradford-on-Avon. I was four and I am not sure if I have many memories of the place that pre-dated our first encounters with the Netleys. I am sure that my mother and father will tell the story of how they met as a result of my sister Collette and Chris attending the same nursery school and Ebet having her leg in plaster and unable to chase after Chris. Dad was volunteered by Mum to go and help Ebet and Brian with work to their kitchen floor. My first memory of the place was a great black hole where the kitchen floor should have been. No-one ever entered the house from the front door and filing through the utility room to look into a dark void made a peculiar impression upon me. It was after the kitchen had been rebuilt as it is now with comforting green cabinets and the pine table re-installed that we really got to know each other and the friendship between our two families grew.

We moved from Bradford to Cricklade in 1973 but the families maintained regular contact, staying weekends at each other's houses or meeting for a pub supper at the Wagon and Horses in Beckhampton.

Ebet had been for most of the time I had known her an alternative mother figure. After my immediate family, she was the adult who I was closest to, and her personality made everyone feel as though they were special to her. Of course as an

78

adult, mother and, soon to be, teacher she was very comfortable being bossy, especially where we children were concerned.

Now, for some reason, Ebet came to driving a bit later than most people these days. For all of our childhood, she did not drive. But in 1983 she bought a white Fiesta van and set about learning. One of the wonderful things about having an alternative family was that I could go and stay with them and for a number of years I had stayed a week or two of the summer holidays with Andy, Chris, Brian and Ebet.

This particular summer was special. I had a car and a licence to drive it. Andy and I had freedom to cruise the streets of Bradford and Bath on a mis-guided and doomed mission to pick up girls. As Ebet was a learner driver and in need of practice and Andy had not yet passed his test, I volunteered to sit with her while she drove the van, with Andy and Chris in the back offering 'encouragement'. I soon realised that for the first time, I knew how to do something Ebet didn't and as far as the law of the road went, I was in charge, the boss! 'Mirror, signal, indicate - Watch your road position – Did you check your shoulder before pulling out then?' This was at direct odds with our relationship up to this point and it took a while for Ebet to get used to this terrible hectoring teenage teacher, in reality she was already pretty good behind the wheel, but she took the change in roles in good part and by the next time we all met up, I had lost my advantage. Ebet had passed her test!

Sitting around the kitchen table at about this

time, I, the moderately rebellious teenager, used to enjoy debating some of the big questions with Ebet. She always treated me as a person with valid opinions even if she disagreed with them. One particular debate centred on the existence of God; my viewpoint was one of a firm agnostic, hers from a position of faith.

'What gets me is this whole, God watches over us all stuff…I mean how is that possible?'

To which Ebet replied, 'I think it works the same way as love. Do you think there are a finite number of people that you can love at one time?'

I'm not sure that I agreed then or now with her view regarding God, but I think it says a lot about the way Ebet was. She was comfortable with who she was and investing time and interest in young people above all, she clearly believed that there was no finite limit to her love and this she shared generously and openly with her family and friends.

Other memories:
- 'Andrew John!' this was how she always spoke to Andy when he did something wrong.
- Slightly overdone Brussels with Sunday lunch – a firm favourite.
- Chatting through the serving hatch from dining room and kitchen while Ebet slaved over the stove.
- Ebet's beautiful coloured ink illustrations for her unpublished alphabet book – X played the Xylophone with his toes.
- Owls and Roman glass.
- Telling us off for making a cardboard bob-

sleigh to ride down the polished wood stairs. Ebet told me that sometimes teachers had to pretend to be cross even if they weren't. She was really cross this time!

- Encouraging me to draw the stone garden wall visible from the living room 'Look at each stone individually, don't just make them up, each has its own character'

- Tolerance of Andy and I playing Heavy Metal in the living room or Chris the 'Flash Gordon' theme song for the 1000th time in a row.

- Playing board games around the dining table; the Netleys always had a new one to play. The best was Sigma File.

- She had a thing for Bob Wilson – former Arsenal goalie and TV sports commentator!

- She told me, while giving us worldly advice, about an old garage sign, that she and a friend had in their flat at college, which read 'Have you had your brakes tested recently?'. A warning for when everything seems to be going too well.

- Ebet reading a lovely poem about Collette my sister at her first wedding – with a cheeky reference to cherry stones that only four of us would get.

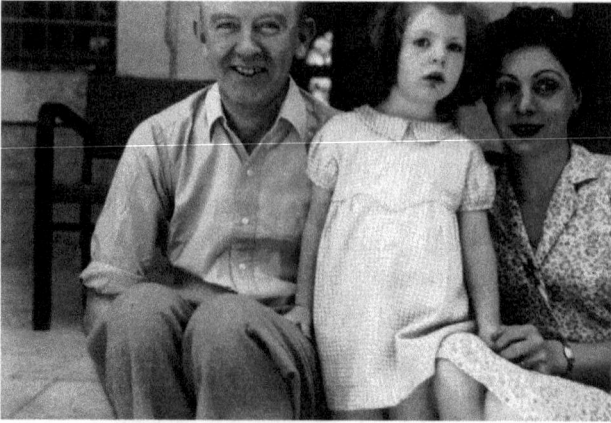

In Palestine with parents 1944

Scotland 1945

Scotland 1946

Brooklands 1955

With Biddy 1958

Pioneer Camp 1959 (2nd. Left)

The 'May' Ball 1961   Southampton Uni' Ball 1962

With friends & partners before the 'May' Ball
1962

Signing the Register 10/8/63

Married!

Wedding Toast

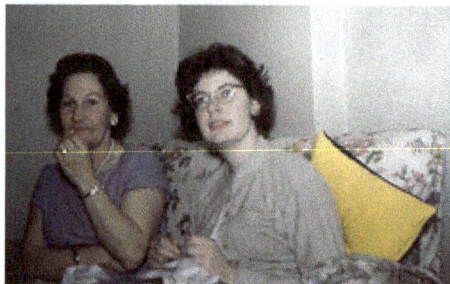

With Brian's mother at Rosemary's 21st. 1961

21st. Birthday at Teacher Training College 1963

With Paul & Philip Hocking 1965

With Brian's family
Christmas 1960

Alison's Christening
1964

Postbridge, Dartmoor, Honeymoon 1963

Portrait 1965

New-born Andy 1966

The Green Dress - July 1966

Victoria Park, Bath 1975

Chris' new bike 1981

The Family 1st January 1985

Homework! Feb. 1985

With Meg, Kangaroo Island, 1986

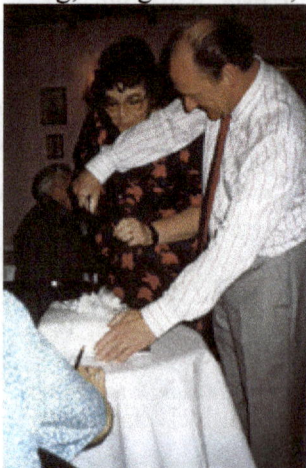

Silver W. Cake (made & brought by Meg from Australia)

Through the Hatch 1995

An S.C.F. 'thank you' at the Wharf, Devizes 1989

In London 1991

Ruby Anniversary 2003

With Friend Janet c. 2000

With Helen, Stewart & Family 1991

IAN AND JANET BACK

were asked to give the Eulogy at Liz's funeral. This is what they said

Ian - We knew Elizabeth as Ebet, a very special friend of ours and of our children, Spencer and Collette, for 40 years.

Janet - Just how do we condense all that time of knowing her into a few minutes? There were so many facets to Ebet that made her the warm and generous person she was.

Ian - For us we remember her passion for owls, as well as other wild life, and of her many collections: glass, china, handbags, pictures and books etc.

Janet - Also, drama played an important part in Ebet's life as both a teacher and a theatre goer, as well as her love of literature.

Who could forget the wonderful creations she made of jewellery, painted rocks, her alphabet book, abstract cartoons of owls and her lovely poems, as well as her creative needlework.

Ian - Ebet was always very enthusiastic, supportive and encouraging for everything we undertook, whether it was renovating a house or our arts and crafts endeavours. As a measure of her support and humour, I remember an occasion when I was having difficulties with a work colleague, she offered to go and bop him on the nose for me.

Janet - She had a great sense of humour, full of laughter and would always look for the amusement in a situation – but we can not forget that when she wanted to, she could enjoy a good debate too!

Ian - Her friendship enriched our lives immensely and we will always miss her, as I'm sure everyone here will.

Janet - It's been a privilege to have had her as our friend. Goodbye, God bless you, dear Ebet.

The Celebration of Liz's life
ANN HOLLAND

This took place in Holy Trinity Church on Thursday 13th January and was very well attended with families and friends of Liz and Brian coming from various parts of the country to pay their respects. The Rev. Bill Matthews and Jean drove down from near Newark and many old friends were reunited in a way that would have warmed Liz's heart.

Reflections on Liz's life were read by Liz and Brian's sons, Chris and Andy. Also tributes were paid by Janet and Ian Back. The prayers of intercession were led by Chris Hodge and the address was given by The Revd Joanna Abecassis.

Familiar hymns, 'The King of Love my

shepherd is' and 'Rock of Ages' were sung, with the choir singing "Lead me Lord" during the giving of communion.

After the commendation and farewell, the dismissal given and the congregation left to the sound of the chorale improvisation on Nun Danket by Siegfried Karp-Elert, played on the organ by Gareth Bennett.

While the private family committal took place at the Bradford on Avon cemetery, the rest of the congregation were invited to St. Margaret's Hall for refreshments and were later joined by the family.

On this day the first snowdrops appeared in Liz's garden.

Leapfrogging over the small children and collapsing in a heap on the grass
MARILYN MAUNDRELL

It is hard to choose the words to include in Brian's book. You were a 'full-of-fun and caring friend' for many years.

I remember being on your garden steps when you arrived at your new home – just across the alley from where Peter and I and Lesley lived. I was always in awe of your many talents – painting, drawing, tapestry, appliqué, wood carving (my favourite carving was the lovely 'owl'). Also your knack of finding just the right thing to buy to go on your shelves amongst dozens of treasures you had on display e.g. glassware, wooden ornaments, pottery, ivory pieces and many small pieces of china.

The souvenirs you brought back from your holidays in this country and abroad were all on display. Every time you came home from your holidays, I would rush down to your house to see what your latest buy was. Your wall hangings, pictures and Chinese masks in your sun-lounge were amazing. You always seemed to bring me a gift as well – our tastes were very similar. I still have your gifts on show around our home and the postcards sent from the places you and Brian and the boys visited.

You would show Chris's amazing drawings of dinosaurs, and other imaginary creatures he would draw for his homework projects.

As for Andrew, he is now still as handsome and achieving so much with his TV documentaries.

The family parties you invited Pete and I to come to were so much fun. The games we would play 'fantastic'.

When Pete and I had a party at French Grass House to celebrate Queen Elizabeth's Silver Jubilee, you and your family and many friends came – sports were played on the lawn – I remember you leapfrogging over the small children and collapsing in a heap on the grass – table tennis in the 'games room' - good food and dancing in the evening.

I've got the silent video films from that day and, as one does, out they come and we watch and laugh at them all over again.

Last but not least was your gift of making your

pupils at school aware of their capabilities – giving them confidence to go forward and achieve; this ended in so many parents seeing their children keen to get into school, instead of dreading going to school. The means which helped all this to happen was drama - it gave the pupils an outlet to freely express their feelings.

Sometimes we would go to Bath, shopping; I would try and persuade you to buy some clothes, but No! No! No! Not interested – you would rather buy new paints or silks for your tapestries. You were always a lovely family, very supportive to each other

'In sickness and in health,' keep an eye on us all, Liz.

The lion tamer
THALIA RACE

Liz was one of the first people I met when we came to live in St. Margaret's Place in October 1971. Always a difficult time when one moves to a new house, Liz welcomed me and my family into the 'alley' and never minded that my children from a house with no TV, spent time in her house glued to the screen.

Apart from being a loyal and highly entertaining friend for nearly 40 years, I will always think of her as the mediator, the counsellor to those living in the alley. She was a good listener and a wise woman. I might even go so far as to call her 'the lion tamer' for her greatest feat in the alley was the taming of Betty Siddall, a spinster and retired secretary. We all thought of Betty as a cantankerous old woman who hated children and would stand on her doorstep hurling abuse at them when they were too noisy. That was until Liz befriended her. I don't know what Liz did but Betty Siddall turned into one of the sweetest of neighbours who took an active interest in the families around her. When she died in 1987 she was sorely missed.

Liz was talented in so many ways. She loved making things. Every Christmas she would present us with a wonderful seasonal gift that she had made. So it has become part of our Christmas ritual to bring out the 'Liz gifts' to decorate our house; the patchwork Christmas tree, the embroidered robin, the string of hearts and the Advent Calendar, to name but a few. Highly imaginative she could tell a good story, put on a good show, writing the script herself and, for The Silver Jubilee Street Party in the alley, she devised a fiendish treasure hunt that had us traipsing up and down St. Margaret's Place.

The last year of Liz's life, when I saw her more frequently, was an inspiration to me. She showed such fortitude and spirit in the face of adversity. A huge fighter, even when in considerable pain, she never seemed to lose her sense of humour, her sense of the ridiculous.

A friendly hint
BETTY SIDDALL
Written by Brian

Betty, a slightly eccentric spinster, lived at 8 St. Margaret's Place, opposite to our garden. Below is a letter from Betty to Ebet dated 1 July 1973.

Dear Mrs Netley,

I'm sure you won't mind a friendly hint (which it is hoped may help - in the problem most parents have with exuberant children!) - about reducing the decibels arising from the garden:- your two plus Number - 5's and Number - 6's - and now Number 7's!

Many of the long-term residents around here and St. Margaret's Villas, and I, are complaining of the noise - especially on Sundays - and although I have only been here 13 years - there are families nearby whose parents and Grandparents are still living here - and are accustomed to quiet neighbours. Sounds carry far, in the country - unless one lives in a house entirely surrounded by fields: it is all much noisier in the South East of England, where there are jet planes, traffic and large housing estates, and of course there are differences in a small West Country town. -As children in this "alley" are strong and healthy and well grown. -It would be such a pity if nice little families became unpopular with long-established residents - and - were allowed to Whoop it up without some correction - and spoil all their splendid possibilities! - I have many nephews and

100

nieces - all "full of go" - but well?!
With kindest regards and good wishes.
(no reply needed.)
Yours sincerely,
Betty Siddall

P.S. I'm sure you won't let your splendid young Tarzan (A) get big-headed, or bullying. He looks wonderfully strong and enterprising, and should be able to help younger-ones, when it's put to him!

I have no record of Ebet's reply to the above letter. What I do remember is that Ebet befriended Betty, to the extent she often joined us for Saturday (I think) tea and watched various TV programmes, such as Cliff Richard and Diane Solomon, with us.

She came to appreciate all the local children and very much joined in when we had the 'Alley Party' to celebrate the Queen's Silver Jubilee.

Betty was a steam railway enthusiast (her father having been a railway engineer) and Ebet encouraged her to take a train holiday, visiting old haunts in the north of England, especially to what were then becoming private railways, following the efforts of Dr. Beeching to destroy our railway system.

The following letter was sent to Ebet from the R.U.H.

Tuesday 23rd December '86

Dearest Lizzoo -

I've been whisked into the <u>Victoria Ward at R.U.H.</u> today - by Dr. Catt!   *(The letter is difficult to read - the gist is that explorations were being carried out on a suspected 'blockage' in her stomach and she expected to be kept in over Christmas. All sorts of messages to be passed on to neighbours. May need an operation, but hopes to be home in about a week.)*

I do hope you will have a very happy Christmas and New Year.

All the best dear, and much love.

Bet. XXXX

My diary records Ebet visiting Betty in R.U.H. several times and again, later, at Bradford Hospital. She spent many hours with Betty during the week leading up to her death on 14 April 1987.

A Kenning
RACHEL OLIVER

Red wearing
Bird watching

Flower loving
Friend keeping

Picture stitching
Laugh making

Card writing
Text sending

An ever listening and empathetic ear
CHRISTOPHER AND KATE SYKES

We moved to Bradford on Avon from London in 1971, taking up residence in a damp and leaky agricultural 'tied' cottage off St Margaret's Steps.

It was in fact Thalia Race, a very near neighbour of Liz's, whom we first befriended in St Margaret's Place. She, cautiously, out of curiosity, crept up some narrow alleyway steps off Bridge Street, straight into our rambling overgrown hillside garden one day. I am not sure who was the more surprised: she or us, but through Thalia inviting us soon afterwards to her house, we very soon spotted Brian and Liz hard at work in their own lovely garden beside a junction of two footpaths, almost opposite Thalia's house, and we

103

quickly made friends with them, too.

Brian, at that stage was hard at work as an accountant and we usually saw more of Liz, when we passed by on our way to Thalia and Bob's home. Straight away, we hit it off. Liz was bubbly, laughing, jokey and full of fun. Through cups of tea in her kitchen or outside on her patio, we were soon introduced to her two sons, Andrew and Christopher, both at school, while Brian, to us, remained somewhat in the background at that time, no doubt very hard pressed with his business commitments, though we passed the time of day on a few occasions. Later on, we got to know him much better.

We also learned, on getting to know the Netleys, that certain family members had some worrying health issues, including Liz, but she always (typically) played down her aches and pains, rejoicing in spontaneous friendship and circumstance, at each meeting. This was so characteristic of a determined battler, who was not going to let (to the outside world, at least) her heart hang too obviously on her metaphorical sleeve, and she would always find some humour and lighter touch to turn aside inner worries and pains so that she did not inflict these issues on others. Similarly, any anxiety over health worries over her children she would honestly admit but never burden others, preferring greatly to show her instinctive and genuine interest in the lives of the friends before her and their own families.

It was immediately apparent that Liz had an ongoing and life-long love affair with nature. She, and Brian, cherished their garden, revealing green fingers in the loving care of her patios and pots in a cleverly laid-out and interesting corner garden, visibly on show to all passing pedestrians; and she took a lively interest in those Bradford neighbours who passed by her doors, with an ever listening and empathetic ear cocked to the concerns and worries of her friends and acquaintances. Such meetings would invariably turn from serious matters into irrepressible giggles before very long.

Another talent of Liz's was manifest from early on; her great and deep creative skills with both art and crafts. Her home became a treasure house of unusual taste and objects d'art, and our eyes would wander around the crowded and competing shelves, coffee tables and walls, savouring the many unexpected artistic delights of a very creative and industrious person. She had the natural magpie mind of a collector with a keen eye for the unusual. But much of this artwork was her own, and it reflected Brian's and her own very catholic taste and love of bold and colourful designs, fabrics, wood carving, pottery and pictures.

She was delightfully 'touchy feely' with people she knew and liked. On one occasion, Chris and Liz exchanged some lively creative writing on the subject of the wonderful Pandora's Box which her living room represented in Chris's mind, and Liz's robust poem written in reply was sheer brilliance, causing side-splitting laughter at this end.

Liz showed enormous interest in Kate's art work, not only by her warm and enthusiastic approval but by offering to market it for Kate, which, no doubt, had the opportunity arisen, she would have done with all the amazing energy she always found when helping others to achieve their potential. This, we think, was one of her greatest qualities, revealing a generous and overflowing heart.

Liz's talent for amateur dramatics was something we only learned about much later on, when her prowess as an inspiring teacher led to a fine reputation in the schools she taught in, including Lavington Comprehensive, not far from us, where her acolytes included Ben Johns and David Pinson. This fact became known to us during our Edington years through our own deep friendship with the boys' parents. Indeed, Liz was a veritable Miss Jean Brodie in her charisma, vision and passionate belief in honest committed education, fought for valiantly, despite conservative opposition from some sceptical teaching colleagues, on occasions. This forthrightly expressed honest opinion inevitably led to one or two clashes with colleagues, but this did not deter Liz one iota as she fought for her own and her pupils' best interests and useful resources. This unswerving commitment in her work-life produced many fine drama productions.

Back at home, we fondly remember those occasional candlelit evening meals with Brian and Liz in their comfortable and stylish home, and some pretty late (and dare I say it?) boozy totters back home down St Margaret's Steps in the small hours!

We were well aware of their later passion for holidaying in their motor home. Who could not notice the tidily parked large van peeping over the dry-stone wall as one passed by along the Strips woodland path back to Greenland View? We had moved here for a further three years before leaving Bradford altogether, heading for Edington, our next house venue, where we have resided ever since (amounting to some 35 years, to date!). Clearly, the Netley's travelled extensively, together, on welcome breaks when time allowed.

Liz's latter-day battles with arthritis and then cancer in her arm, and eventually elsewhere in her body, were an inspiration in courage set against adversity, and her grim and latterly dark sense of humour was never extinguished. Through gritted teeth at her Warminster Hospital bedside, she could still crack a joke, albeit in a fuzzy haze of drugged pain. She never let on any inward sense of despair or hopelessness, even though she must have heard the approaching tramp of the end. I cannot now recall in-depth discussions on personal faith with Liz, but feel sure that this many-sided woman, who revealed so many talents to her loyal friends, would have met her Maker, eyeball to eyeball, in complete honesty, for this is the person we all knew and loved.

Her legacy was revealed to all at her memorial service at Holy Trinity Church to a packed congregation where tributes and anecdotes flowed freely from all sectors of the Bradford on Avon community, and afterwards in St Margaret's Hall for the meal celebration.

She has left two fine sons, one in variable health who battles on just like his mother did, and both with huge love and respect for their much missed mother, while, for Brian, this must have been a shattering experience, even though he (and Lizzie) could see it coming from quite far off. Brian never lost hope and his love and close support to Liz in those dark last days was evident to all.

Hopefully, these few words, inadequate though they must be, coming from a relatively fringe quarter, will stir one or two more memories for the reader. Certainly, they are offered with all sincerity and love, and I apologize if some details are by now a bit fuzzy and far off. In our hearts Liz lives on, bold and funny, friendly and zany, and always vital and interesting. It has been a pleasure and privilege to have known her for as long as we did.

An extremely good listener
CHRISTINE DUCAT

I have known Liz since 1979 when we first met, quite accidentally, at the Royal United Hospital in Bath. Both our sons, both called Andrew, were patients in the hospital. I was, I suppose, visibly upset and worried about my son, especially as I was a lone parent. Liz saw my distress and came up and put her arms round me; a particularly comforting gesture, although we were still strangers to one another.

We thereafter became close friends for all the years that followed, up until her death. We had many jolly jaunts together in her red car of which she was very fond.

One of the great things about Liz for me was her marvellous and constant encouragement; she was like St Barnabas in the bible. She, as an artist herself, was really the first person who gave me faith in myself as an artist. She even provided the wine for the private view of my first solo exhibition at Bath University.

She continued to spur me on, but allowed me enough space in which to recover from a double bereavement when it was quite impossible for me to paint. After that lengthy period of time, she encouraged me to hold another solo exhibition, this time at the Black Swan Gallery in Frome.

Also, Liz was an extremely good listener – always prepared to listen even when feeling unwell, which was most of the time in later years.

She was a great source of support for me, especially when my son was ill.

Liz was extremely generous – my house holds many gifts from her, including a most beautiful hand stitched tapestry cushion and a tapestry sampler - work which must have taken many, many hours of painstaking stitching.

She always sent me postcards whilst she and Brian were away on holiday and she never forgot my birthday. She even gave me a proper birthday cake one year, something I have missed over the years, having my birthday on Christmas day.

Liz greatly encouraged me in my newly found

Christian faith – she came to my confirmation in Bath Abbey, a very special time for me.

All in all Liz was a very special, loving and most lovable friend, much missed.

I shall always remember her with gratitude.

A very special place in our hearts
SUE AND GRAHAM

We first met Liz in 1991 when we moved to Wiltshire and our daughters attended Lavington School. Our youngest daughter Ali did drama and soon became very attached to this lovely teacher, who was a great mentor for many students.

We really got to know Liz and Brian as friends the following year when our eldest daughter Karen mentioned that a boy called Dan, in her year, was to go home to Australia due to family commitments. He did not want to go and wanted to complete his education in the UK. At this time he was due to go into his final year at Lavington and take GCSE's. He wondered if anyone would be willing to look after him.

Having moved to Wiltshire the year before and not really wanting to be here, we knew how he felt so, after having a family conference, we said if everyone was in agreement we would be prepared to have him live with us. Liz was very instrumental in this and with a lot of help from her it was arranged for him to come and live with us. She could see the potential in him that the other teachers could not, and he has not let her down.

He lived with us for eight months, took his exams and then went home to Australia where he has settled really well with a very good job and a lovely wife (we attended their wedding in Australia in September 2007). We keep in touch and would love to go back to visit again.

We all have a very special place in our hearts for Liz and I don't think Dan would be the person he is today if she had not had the faith in him.

We have kept in touch ever since with Liz and Brian, we were invited to join them for their special 40th wedding celebrations.

Dan adds:-

I suppose for me, at that age and with all the confusion and turmoil with my family, it was the first time in my life that I was able to see a teacher as someone to trust and count as a friend. I really felt that Liz wanted the best for me and was interested in helping me to understand my own self-worth, the importance in valuing myself and realising that my own expectations of my potential were the most important.

Liz helped me take steps towards understanding that my happiness was something I could control and it did not need to be based on others' opinions or view of me.

As mentioned, she was also instrumental in bringing Sue, Graham and their family into my life.

I believe that because of her involvement, I was able to realise that, from that moment until now, I have always been surrounded by the most magnificent people in my life, who have such a positive and strengthening effect on me and my well-being, and that must be partly due to who I am, and I credit some of that to Liz's influence and friendship.

Memories of a friend
VAL PAWLYN
Written by Brian

Val came to Bradford from Cornwall in about 1997, together with husband Tony and children Neil and Catherine. Neil and Andy were about the same age, as were Catherine and Chris. It was Tony's work that brought the family to this area.

Liz and Val soon struck up a very close friendship. Besides our joint social activities, Liz and Val had common interests in sewing and the like; and also difficult family backgrounds.

Tony's work took the family further west after about five years, when they lived just west of Exeter. A few more years and it was back to Cornwall living near Truro.

We visited them wherever they were, including for Catherine's marriage in 1990, and they came to us several times, especially for celebrations of Silver and Ruby weddings. A visit we made in 1988 included our great friend Meg O'Brien.

Val made us a beautifully embroidered tapestry for our Silver wedding and many other handmade cards etc over the years.

Val was hospitalised in 2005 and contracted some disease in the hospital which caused her untimely death. Liz was distraught but there was little we could do, especially as Liz had her own medical problems. Tony became rather reclusive, but we kept in touch with daughter, Catherine.

It was letters and 'phone calls on a regular basis
THE O'BRIENS
Written by Brian

When I was 'doing' my National Service, I was posted to Singapore, arriving in April 1959. Several members of our Corps (RAPC) attended St. Georges Church, Tanglin, which was the main Forces church in Singapore. Non-forces people also used that church, among them the O'Brien family (John, who was attached to the Australian Trade Mission, Meg, his wife and Julia and Bob, their children), who made a point of inviting members of the forces, far from their homes, to visit their home for refreshment and company. I was very fortunate to be invited.

About 6 months after arriving in Singapore, I was posted to Ipoh in N. Malaya, attached to 13/18 Hussars. For Christmas 1959 I stayed at Sandy's Home (for Forces' personnel) in Singapore and was part of a large celebration on the verandah of the O'Brien's home on Christmas Day. After this I stayed with the family on several occasions, including the few days prior to repatriation and demob at the end of October 1960.

I kept in touch with the family through correspondence. In 1972 my parents took a 'round-the-world' cruise which, of course, included Australia. Arrangements were made for my parents to leave the ship at Sydney, where they were met by Meg and John to be taken to their home in Canberra. They then rejoined the ship at Melbourne.

Meg and John visited England in 1984, on their way from the U.S.A. to continental Europe. They only stayed for 2 nights. We took them to Lacock, where everyone was having a great time, including the Morris Dancers. We had to drive through them very slowly and somehow I got vibes from John - I said "would you like to get out?" – and he was gone!

What luck to go there on that day.

John subsequently wrote a letter about it to Andy and Chris. If we weren't friends before, we certainly were after that visit. Sadly John died a few months later.

Ebet became great friends with Meg; there must be 100 letters from Meg in my file.

In 1986, Ebet and I had our first long-distance holiday, visiting Singapore, Queensland including a short stay with Bob O'Brien and his family, Canberra (stayed with Meg's cousin June and husband Tom), Adelaide (where Meg now lived), Perth (Jenny and Brian) and Bangkok.

In 1988, Meg came to stay with us for our Silver Wedding celebration, and brought with her a beautiful anniversary cake. Whilst with us, she borrowed Ebet's car to visit other friends.

Then, in 1990, we went to Australia again, spending a few days in Sydney and then to Meg's home. From there we hired a 4-wheel drive vehicle and the three of us explored northern S.Australia, including The Flinders ranges, Lake Eyre South, Woomera etc. What an adventure!

The last time we saw Meg was in 1994, when she came to stay for several weeks and joined us for a holiday in Northumberland and Shropshire and places in between.

From then until Meg's death it was letters and 'phone calls on a regular basis.

We also had the pleasure of several visits by Julia, with whom Ebet carried on the letter habit. Julia continues with her memories.

Age was no factor in the friendships she forged.
JULIA ARCHER

For years before I knew Liz Netley, she was my mother's good friend. The fact Liz and I also became good friends is an indication that age was no factor in the friendships she forged.

Liz and Brian came out to Australia more than once, and had adventures with my mother, Meg O'Brien, in the outback with a 4-wheel drive and on Kangaroo Island. I have photos of them on the beach with sea lions and exploring out-of-the-way distinctly Australian landscapes.

My mother had always had nostalgia for the

UK, which she had never visited, and through her friendship with Liz and Brian she was able to discover England and go on many wonderful sightseeing trips. They showed her their favourite places, and brought her so much joy in all the memories they gave her.

My mother talked to the end of her life of prehistoric sites, villages, teashops, rural landscapes, of Bradford on Avon and many happy hours in the Netley home laughing and talking.

She and Liz also wrote and phoned each other faithfully for decades.

When I finally visited England for the first time I received the same welcome and saw some of the places of which my mother had talked so fondly. I was the beneficiary of Liz and Brian's knowledge and love of little byways and secret jewels.

Even in the summer of 2009, when Liz was far from well, she took me to some of her favourite haunts like All Saints, Great Chalfield and Wells Cathedral. There were visits to bookshops and teashops and rural drives past thatched houses, as we chatted and laughed and she told me about birds and wildflowers.

Liz was an active and wise listener when conversation turned to the personal. Whether it was help with my creative writing or with my struggles as a governess teaching children in a very remote location, or talking about family, Liz had time to listen and offered shrewd insights and practical suggestions. I valued this more than I can ever say.

Having been a nomad all my life, I don't have a

great many friendships which go back years and stay strong. Liz was one of the few, and one of the very few who also knew my mother.

Her passing has left an empty place. I miss her cards, emails and letters, her just being *Liz*.

All from a cup of tea!
FRED AND PAOLA SAUNDERS
Written by Brian

In about 1976, Ebet was walking with the boys in the Country Park on a Sunday afternoon. They met a couple of visitors from America, who asked Ebet if she knew where they could get a cup of tea. In those days, not many such places were open in Bradford on a Sunday. She invited them to come home with her, which they did.

He was Fred Saunders, a University lecturer from New York State and she was Sue Dietrich, his sister in law from Chicago. Apparently, Fred had arranged the trip with his wife but when she died Sue agreed to accompany him so that he would not miss out on his only visit to England. They were staying with friends at Marshfield.

There followed correspondence with both Fred and Sue. Fred married again, to Paola, and they visited this area some years later, again staying with their friends in Marshfield.

Several times they invited us to visit their home in Cornwall-on-Hudson, which we eventually did in the summer of 1987. We spent a week or so with them, being shown around the area, including a visit to Manhattan (I had to park the car for Fred!) We also took the train into the city on our own on another day. Paola and Fred then took us to stay with friends at Marblehead, north of Boston. This was another lovely visit, including trips out on their friend's yacht, one of which was to greet a British chap, James Hatfield, who was sailing round the world single-handed to raise funds for the BHF. This included the fire-tenders with their great spouts of water.

Paola and Fred returned home and Ebet and I hired a car and did a five day tour of New England before returning home via Boston and New York.

Fred died in the mid-nineties but Paola is still going strong, making occasional visits to Europe, including Bradford on Avon. We continue to correspond. All from a cup of tea!

She was always surrounded by an entranced group of people
AUDREY TINKLER

My husband and I met Liz and Brian on a cruise in the Aegean 11 years ago and it was an instant rapport with both of them, which we came to treasure.

Wherever Liz was on the ship "Minerva" she was always surrounded by an entranced group of people and we were delighted to be welcomed into their company so quickly. Afterwards Liz's warmth and charisma were a joy whenever we met, especially as I shared fibromyalgia with her

118

and we could say "ouch" together!

We also shared a love of embroidery and spent many hours admiring each other's work. Her output was twice the size of mine, however, and I was frequently amazed at the beautiful things she produced so quickly – usually to give away to somebody.

Sadly I didn't have many years to enjoy Liz's company, and I don't know much about her life before we met; but as a retired teacher like Liz I could imagine how brilliant and beloved she was in her professional life by the experiences she shared with me.

I asked her to say a few words at our Diamond Wedding party at the Priory Hotel in Bath and the following is what she said. John and I were both deeply moved by it and it reflects both her warmth and her way with words so I kept a copy of it.

"When I was at college, (many hundreds of years ago!) I was told that people who could spell visualised the word, and people who couldn't spell visualised what the word meant. Well I can't spell so I saw everything in pictures. So when I hear "Audrey and Johnnie" I have a very specific picture in my head, and it's of Audrey in John's arms waltzing on the Swan Hellenic "Minerva" while we were in the Aegean sea, and they both looked so elegant – Audrey beautiful and John very handsome – but the main thing was how comfortable they looked together and how very happy. And isn't it fantastic that after 60 years they still look so happy and comfortable and so much in love and that is something to celebrate.

And so I'd like to say not only 'Congratulations', but 'Thank you', because the warmth and affection spill over, and I'm sure everybody here feels very privileged to know you."

She was such a life-enhancer and I miss her so much.

Wicked sense of humour
PHYLLIS AND ROBIN FEWINGS

Phyllis and I did not know Liz for any great length of time – our friendship emerged bit by bit as the years rolled by, but the more we got to know her, the more we valued her friendship (and Brian's of course)

Brian became County Treasurer for Wiltshire Scouts in 1999 and, as a Chartered Accountant, was always a stickler for "the rules of accounting"! Our paths crossed from time to time during the next three years and then the frequency of meetings increased as I had volunteered to raise the necessary funds to modernise the County Scout Centre at Potterne Wick, near Devizes.

The target was £700,000 and Brian agreed to assist with completing the many applications forms required by the potential funders. Various meetings were held, some of which were at Brian's house in Bradford on Avon. As a result of this, Phyllis and I met Liz and began to be aware of what a splendid person she was. She was always merry and bright, despite being in a great deal of pain because of her various medical problems.

The friendship between us blossomed such that we had meals together, sometimes in our houses and sometimes in a wonderful French restaurant in Bath. My wife and I became aware of Liz's wicked sense of humour and her readiness to 'go to the barricades' for her friends. If we said that someone was being difficult, Liz would offer to go and biff them on the nose! And she meant it!

She followed our fundraising progress with keen interest, occasionally offering helpful suggestions as to the best way forward. She was particularly supportive when our two applications to the National Lottery were rejected. "Never mind," she said, "You will get there in the end - I know you will." Her faith in our eventual success was unswerving. We did 'get there in the end', although it took nearly five years.

One of her greatest skills was in knowing, through years of experience as a teacher, how young people thought and acted. We had the opportunity to apply for funding to the Wiltshire Young People's Opportunity Fund – a fund administered by the County Council. Phyllis and I were visiting Liz and Brian and I was explaining to them that this funding had to be applied for by the young people who would benefit from it.

"This is what you must do," said Liz. "You must find a group of scouts; provide them with copies of the application form; explain clearly what the funding is for and then let them get on with it. Don't worry about the grammar or the spelling – just let them do it their way."

I was very dubious but thought that, since I had asked her, I had best take her advice. Otherwise she would give me one of her "Grrrs"!

We 'borrowed' nine young scouts from the County's contingent to the Centenary World Scout Jamboree and asked them to carry on. They did, and the result was a cheque for £50,000! We subsequently used the same technique with a different group of scouts and realised a further £15,000. How wise you were, Liz.

Phyllis and I visited Liz in hospital several times, both in Bristol and in Warminster and saw the same determination, courage and sense of humour, despite her knowing that she didn't have much time left. She was worried about Brian and their son, Christopher and how they would manage without her. She was far more worried about them than herself.

What a lady! Aren't we lucky to have known her?

Her observations were remarkably sagacious
ANN HOLLAND

Liz and I first became friendly when we were part of a small group of people making monthly recordings of the Holy Trinity Parish News for the visually impaired members of our congregation. This was around 2007/8.

The recordings were made in the house of an elderly gentleman who was a technical expert and

Liz and I would speculate about what the neighbours thought when several ladies emerged from his house after a couple of hours, chuckling and joking, having imbibed the odd glass or two of the host's wine. Liz referred to us as 'Dennis's harem'!

Liz and I shared interests in wild life and teaching drama and because of her delightful sense of fun we had lots of laughs.

Liz started to write a Nature Diary for Parish News while I was a co-editor and her observations were remarkably sagacious with frequent touches of humour.

Interested in other people and their worlds
MICHAEL MANSER

By the time I met Liz she was in the midst of her many problems and concerns connected with her health. Nevertheless, in my sadly few meetings with Liz she seemed so constructive, interesting and, what is rarer, interested in other people and their worlds.

Typical I think is that following a visit to John and my house where she learned my family connections with the White Star Line she wrote to me on 4 July 2009, saying, "Do you remember on our visit discussing with John how so many things are linked and inter-connected? Well - I have just re-read a copy of the original 'Just So Stories '- and there, just after the story "The Crab that Played with the Sea" was the enclosed piece.

I copied it out as I thought you may be interested. The piece she so thoughtfully copied and sent to me includes the lines "Or a White Star were to try a Little trip to Surabaya".

As you see, I've treasured her letter and the Rudyard Kipling poem she copied for me.

Eternally helpful and concerned for others around her
CHRIS MILLMAN

I have many memories of Liz and certainly learnt a great deal from her from my contact with her in my role as a Sarcoma Clinical Nurse Specialist.

She was always cheerful and accepting of everything she went through, which was a great deal, she watched and listened to everything around her and was eternally helpful and concerned for others around her.

Brian was a constant support as well as concern for Liz, she always considered him in any decisions and was concerned how he would manage whilst she spent long spells in hospital.

Liz could also be forthright when needed and was able to help improve care given to patients by providing an insight for staff into life as a "patient". She was also great fun and had a wicked sense of humour.

I will always remember her fondly.

Ebet had a very strong Christian faith
BRIAN

Elsewhere there is information regarding the background and roots of Ebet's mother, Elizabeth Beatrice Bowden. This seems to indicate that she was born a Jew. To my knowledge this was never referred to within the family. I do know that Betty was very reluctant to attend any services in church and often complained that church did nothing for her. She requested that there be no religious content at her funeral.

Ebet's father, Godfrey Butler Simmins, was the only child of J F Simmins, a minister of the Episcopal church. The father of J F Simmins and his brother, Godfrey's Uncle William, were also ministers of the Episcopal Church.

It is possible that Godfrey was unaware of Betty's Jewish background.

Ebet and her brother Bill were probably introduced to Christianity in their early years spent in Scotland. Bill was baptised in St Luke's Episcopal Church, Glasgow, on 4th October 1939, and Ebet was baptised in St George's Cathedral, Jerusalem, on 29th August 1942. Both were confirmed into the Anglican church. Interestingly, they both attended the Roman Catholic schools for the major part of their basic education.

Ebet often said she was bullied in school, because she was born in Jerusalem. She had a lifelong hatred of prejudice, particularly religious prejudice. Some of her drama teaching was based on this, with particular reference to prejudice against Jews during the 20th century, throughout the world and particularly in Europe.

Ebet had a very strong Christian faith and practised Christian values throughout her life. I have found it interesting to read that several contributors mention how Ebet's faith affected their own.

She went on collecting to the end
BRIAN

A few years after moving to Bradford on Avon, perhaps 1973/4, Ebet visited a small antiques shop in Church Street (Mrs. Slater). She was quite taken by a pair of cranberry 'dolphin' glasses. She couldn't afford them (a few pounds), so it was agreed she could put a deposit on them and make weekly payments until the total cost was achieved.

From that small beginning, Ebet became very interested in coloured glass items, especially as they looked so good displayed in our 'glass' wall. Her interests in lovely things expanded to include those made of almost any material, especially where skilled techniques had been employed. Her collecting included paintings, etchings, woodcuts, ceramics, ivory, wood-carvings, bronzes and BOOKS!

This brings me to her most important collection - Friends. Ebet seemed able to make friends very easily and she went on collecting to the end. This is what led me to suggest writing a book about her, because all these friends had stories to tell, which I

126

knew little about.

Of course, I was drawn into the collecting 'bug'; and it helped when Ebet wanted to buy me presents (almost any pretext!). I got interested in paintings (we visited many galleries together), boxes, clocks and watches, walking sticks and canes, and brass; also bronzes and books. The friend collecting was also good for me, not being as sociable as Ebet. I'm so thankful I was one of her early 'friend' acquisitions.

One of Ebet's biggest collections is of owls, (must be at least a hundred), but nearly all of these were bought by friends and family. For some reason the idea got around in the early days that she collected owls, so they arrived from all quarters, made of all sorts of materials and in all shapes and sizes. DUSTING!

Our house is called Owlshoot and is still stuffed full of beautiful things and reminders of Ebet's enthusiasms and skills.

She loved creating something special
BRIAN

Friends Issy and Peter came to stay recently. At breakfast (in the kitchen) one morning Issy mentioned a pot on the window sill, holding various implements. She said she thought Ebet had made it at college. I was quite surprised, so removed the implements and examined the pot. Sure enough, the name Simmins was inscribed on the inside of the base (it being a slab pot, so I'm told). It must have been in our homes since we married and either I didn't know Ebet had made it or I had forgotten.

This has led me to think about all the various arts and crafts Ebet indulged in throughout her life.

From quite early, she made cartoon-like drawings of animals and people. She was still making them, until shortly before she died.

When she was about 8 years old, two great-aunts taught her to paint flowers etc. on to porcelain. I have two pieces, one dated 1950 and the other dated 1952.

Ebet would often create a card by painting or drawing in various mediums an illustration suitable to the person and/or the occasion; I expect that many of them are still treasured. She also made many Christmas presents for family and friends, usually a different theme each year. This was not done for economic reasons; she just loved creating something special. She also painted on collected stones and made items from various fabrics, often with a sewn image.

For a year or two she attended evening classes in wood carving. Her best item was an owl.

When she retired, Ebet turned to embroidery and tapestry work. Again, many friends and family members will have some treasured item. I have quite a few in our home. During this time Ebet coped with various physical problems, always trying to find a way around any difficulties.

Ebet much appreciated the 'Arts and Crafts' period of design. One of her favourite designers was William de Morgan, particularly his ceramic tiles, copies of some of which she worked as tapestries. She also created a tapestry based on one of my photos.

We should not, of course, forget Ebet's writings. In her work, she wrote copious lesson notes (all in longhand) and numerous scripts for drama, including adaptations of well-known plays. She also wrote many poems or verse for special occasions or to cheer up somebody. Ebet was also adept at writing to those in authority, when the occasion demanded, most likely on behalf of somebody she considered had been affronted or ill-used.

I'm sure there are many things I have forgotten, but at least I've tried to give a flavour of her industry, especially in 'the arts'.

Ebet behind the wheel
BRIAN

I first owned a car in 1961, when already courting Ebet.

In 1962 I bought a new MG Midget (a heater was extra) - white with red upholstery.

Ebet took out a provisional licence, probably in 1963, and I gave her some rudimentary lessons.

In 1964 I sold the Midget and bought a (white) Sunbeam Alpine from my brother Robin. It was in this car Ebet failed her first driving test (a terrible skid in some high street). Ebet failed a further test. She then became more concerned with motherhood.

In about 1983 I bought a second-hand (white) van for Ebet and she obtained her full licence in August 1983.

Liz described the experience thus:

5th August 1983
I turned off the engine and turned. I knew I'd done it - I must have - surely there was no way I could have failed again.
There followed a time of questioning.
The examiner smiled a lazy smile. "Well Mrs Netley I'm sure you're pleased."
I kissed him! - My mood of depression, hatred of all those who had that precious piece of paper, had passed. I was now a driver. I was free!

Andy also learned to drive in the van.
About 1985 we bought a new Ford Fiesta (not white) for Ebet, which she kept until 1992, when it was passed onto Chris, because...
In spring 1992, I casually asked Ebet what sort of car she fancied - we were in Devizes and she pointed to a (white) Ford Escort XR3i Convertible. Later enquiries led to her saying red was the colour she liked. Nothing more was said, but when she came home from school on 26 June 1992 (her 50th birthday) there in the yard was a new (red) Ford Escort XR3i, with its hood down and a streamer across the windscreen - 'Happy Birthday'.
Because she was late getting home, when she saw a car there she thought, 'Who is that visiting?'

She just loved the car and her 'street cred' with the pupils shot up. She preferred driving that car to any of mine.

In 2006, Ebet's disability was making it difficult to use a clutch, so we had to find an 'automatic', which also had to be a convertible. The best we could find was the silver Vauxhall Astra. It was a great car, but not as much fun as the XR.

P.S. It was fortunate Ebet passed her test in 1983, because in the December of that year I had my first heart attack and couldn't drive for 6 weeks.

***

'TRUE EASE OF WRITING COMES FROM ART, NOT CHANCE'
Alexander Pope (1688 – 1744)

As well as her many creative talents, Liz also loved to write. Her friends can testify to the many hundreds of letters she wrote over the years. For some years she kept a nature diary and she illustrated the wildlife and flowers herself with beautiful drawings, many of them coloured.

Amusing everyday incidents in the home or at work would inspire her to take up a pen to record the event, either in prose or as a poem.

On the 25th anniversary of Liz and Brian's marriage, there was 'open house' in Bradford on Avon, and a weekend of great celebration to which family and friends were all invited. Unfortunately, Brian's parents were unable to attend because of health problems. Liz could not bear them to be left out and, during the weekend, amidst all the organisation and visitors, the cooking and entertaining, she wrote a series of letters in instalments describing the festivities.

Letter 1 (received by Dad on 16/8/88)
Dear Dad (and of course Mum - though I'm sending it to Dad to keep him quiet about me not writing) ----

Anyways
Dear Dad,
Before commencing on the tale of the anniversary deeds the story of the golden orf(e).

We have a golden orfe - what is a fish about as long as this page *(A4)* - as long mind, not as wide - and we've had this here fish for about 5 years. Yesterday we noticed it had a growth around its mouth and Brian pronounced, in words of doom - 'it's going to die'. Today I went to the pet shop and enquired if they had any expertise in golden orfes - 'take it to the vet' they said - it's a valuable fish - 'or better still to an expert in Devizes'.

I decided on the vet, and rang.

"Oh ar" said the receptionist. "I'm not much up on orfes - but bring it down now". *(about 200 yds. away)*.

Twenty minutes later - very wet, I have the Orfe in a large carrier - clear plastic bag and get down to the end of the alley when the orfe turns upside down and stops breathing. Panic - but having watched 'Jaws 3' I know what to do - give it the equivalent of the kiss of life. I dropped to one knee - turned the fish right way up and massaged its gills - great - for all of 5 seconds - then it went wrong way up. I ran all the way home and put it in the pond - where I swear it grinned at me and swam away - leaving me exhausted.

I rang the vet.

"Oh ar" said the receptionist 'that sounds fun!'

Anyways, my golden orfe is now going to have a house call from the vet tomorrow. 'Mind you' said the receptionist darkly 'if anything should happen meantime - you'll let us know won't you'.

I felt like telling her to something orfe!!!

Looks like you'll have to wait till tomorrow

now for dark deeds of anniversary doing.

Much love

   Lizzie poohs!

Letter 2 (received by Dad on 17/8/88)

Dear Dad (and Mum etc!)

On Thursday celebrations began. Having been determined to be very laid back about the whole affair - despite having declared open house Friday, Saturday and Sunday - I ambled off (not orfe-note) shopping and slung immense amounts of food in a shopping trolley. I was just beginning to feel exhausted when Bri turned up. 'Great,' I thought, 'I'll have help!' - Ha Ha!

'I'll catch you up' says Brian - he's getting the drinks. I've just loaded the last item into the last box and put it in the trolley when Bri turns up - I have to load his trolley too, 'cos he's got to find identification of who he is - I told them he belonged to me but they looked very disbelieving - and I've shopped there 17 years!

No Andrew by the way ('I'll be around Thursday and Friday to help'!)

4ish Helen and Stewart (with their two kids who are our godchildren) turn up, plus a tree. Helen's from Carlisle now (Yorkshire originally) and they've been to Wisley and bought us a dwarf tree (about 5ft tall!) which have been travelling with. They had to unload a whole weeks luggage from the car to disembark(!) the tree - it's a Salix Helvetica by the way has catkins and silver foliage in the spring - but can't find it in any book.

134

Then Issy and Peter and one daughter (other one coming the next day) come. I was at college with Helen and Issy, and Stewart and Peter - their husbands are good friends too. They have invited us for a meal at their lodgings and up we go to meet them at 8pm.

The couple running The Round House (where Issy and Helen and co are staying) follow an 'alternative life style' ie they're into vegetarianism and ethnic cultures so they give us a Mexican vegetarian meal - even the 'undressed salad' was hot - chilies with everything!! Stewart and I decided that we had enough hot air between us to lift off a hot-air balloon or kill bats with a single gasp - you must understand that we had had to drink a lot of wine to kill the pain of the Chili <u>non</u> Carne (no meat!!).

Anyways, next day - Issy, Peter, Mary Jane, Stewart, Helen, Neil and Kerina are met in town by Bri and I. We agree to have Mary Jane (who's a bright and beautiful 16 year old) while the rest look around Bradford. 2 hours later Peter arrives with a huge boxful of cream cakes - yum (and flowers). They all stay for lunch and lie sleepily around till Bri persuades them to go for a walk.

(By the way Issy, Peter, Kerina and Helen had already met Bri and I and Meg for early morning service at Saxon Church - yes this was a Friday).

Anyways - next instalment tomorrow.

He he!

Love

Lizzie X

PS - had the house call from the vet - they're

going to tranquillize my poor orfe, examine and operate! Maybe tomorrow - ah!! *(Brian adds - Eventually we had a vet's bill for £29 - a lot of money in those days. The orfe did not live much longer.)*

Letter 3(Received 18/8/88)
Dear Dad (and Mum of course)
        While Bri was out, Val (from Cornwall) turns up - with the most beautiful framed sampler showing our names and dates etc. - gorgeous. She doesn't stay long, (she had actually arrived when Bri was herding the others off but had hid 'cos she was shy!) - anyway - then Pam and her husband Bob came (Bri used to work with Pam when he was 16) and then we had a huge discussion as to whether to have a barbecue - after Bri chickened out and Peter/Stewart etc. had rebuilt the brick one Bri had made - they decided not to - so we made arrangements they should all come back at 7.30 and they went off at 5.
    I cooked supper and then we all ate it. There was Bri and I, Chris and Andy, - (who had finally come 'to help' at 3 - to be fair I worked him like mad once he came - must have made 2,000 cups of tea etc.!) Andrea, Meg, my Mum, Peter, Issy, Mary Jane, Stewart, Helen, Neil, Kerina, Pam and Bob - later Katie (Issy's other daughter) came and we played Trivial Pursuits till 1 a.m.'ish. I lost!!
    Saturday dawned - I went shopping - somehow the immense amount of food had got depleted (what with 11 for lunch and 16 for supper on

Friday) and nothing happened - nobody came!! Peace. Rosemary rang and Bri persuaded her to get Ali to come on the train. Peace still reigned. 5pm - Bri meets Ali off the train. Peace still reigns - Ali, Bri and I and Meg chat peacefully, then at about 6'ish, Barbara, Roy, Sharon, Derek, Rosemary, Keith, Simon, then Mark, Janet, Ian, Spencer, Danny and Biddy all arrived literally within 5 minutes of each other - Mayhem - then, the kettle has a nervous breakdown - Chris comes home - Bri stands in the kitchen muttering 'I can't cope - I'm underwhelmed!!' I put saucepans of water on the cooker and kick the kettle and serve cake. Barbara asks if Mark can spend the night - I say (while dispensing cake) he can have a bit of lounge floor - (at that time we thought we were already sleeping 11).

I try and open pressies and make more tea and dish out cake - Bri longs for bed - Roy - bless him - takes Derek for a walk round town (and I think Mark) - Barbara needs to change - it's now 7 - and I'm in trousers and due down at the Riverside Club at 7.15. We finally chuck out all those who actually have somewhere else to go to, change - Andy and Andrea arrive - tell Chris not to change till everyone else is ready then to lock up - feel bad 'cos we've asked Jan and Ian to come early so we could have a quiet chat!! 7.10 I go to change. 7.15 I'm ready!!

Next bulletin tomorrow
All love
Lizzie X

Letter 4 (Received 19/8/88)

Dear Dad (and you're not to feel neglected Mum 'cos of course these letters are for you too - I'm just making a point).

- got down the Riverside Club with me box of pencils and sheets of clues (Julia should have given you a copy, I'll include one just in case).

We had been told that the main bar would be empty - it wasn't - there were all these poor people trying to eat out and had 70 odd people milling round them asking if they grew garlic for their chickens!!

After about 10 minutes I decide to get out in the fresh air - and meet Bri, who's had the same idea - we grin at each other - then more people arrive. I had hoped that the questionnaire would work but had no idea that it would work quite so well. We simply could not get people in to eat - they were too busy finding out whether this person or that wore yellow ski boots!! All through the meal people were still filling in sheets! Barbara decided she was going to win - no end of people tried to bribe me for answers – we (Bri and I) were having a super time - 'cept I kept busting out all over - must be the excitement - or my fat!

We cut the cake - first I carried it all round the tables - was it heavy! - don't know how Meg managed *(bringing the cake from Australia as cabin luggage)* - Bri and I made a right ham-fisted job of cutting it. Andy gave his speech, starting with - 'I've only known my parents since I was born'! Bri gave his speech (you both were specially mentioned). I invited everyone back for

138

drinks afterwards and said the closing time for the competition was 10.45 and that the bar closed at 11.00. Barbara won! Peter was second - we kept having a wonderful time.

Then I kept saying goodbye to people who said "Oh no we're coming up for coffee!" I lost Bri - eventually I dashed up the road and found I couldn't get in - not that the house was locked but there wasn't room for me - it was raining a bit but folk still were chatting outside in the rain - no Brian - he was apparently chatting to someone at the Club and turned round and everyone was gone! I reckon everyone turned up at home to see if 70 odd people could fit in the house!! The kettle was still having a nervous breakdown - all great fun, especially as one of Bill's sons had a dog. Eventually folk drifted off about 1 to 1.30ish. Chaos reigned. Bri had insisted I make puddings 'cos there was only a choice of one at the meal - guess what mob ate them!!

We decided to open our pressies as it wouldn't be the same the next day (well the same day). We 'oohed' and 'aahed' 'cos we had super gifts - Andy went to sleep on the sofa and Chris on the floor - and we went to bed about 2 and talked til 3.

Next instalment tomorrow.

Lizzie poohs!XX

PS. Bri gave a super speech too and you two were mentioned - he did v.well - proud of all my fellers on the night - so would you have been!

Letter 5 (The final letter)

Dear Dad (and Mum) this is the last instalment - so don't expect another epistle tomorrow - me arms are all wore out!

I had said that we had open house on Sunday so had to get up early to clear the chaos and remove sleeping bodies - Mark had gone the night before with Rosemary, and several other people hadn't stayed so there weren't too many extras. Andy and Andrea were going to Paris so left bleary-eyed but early. Chris got up from the lounge floor and went to bed!!

9.45 Marilyn came whizzing up on her scooter. 9.00 Issy, Peter, Mary Jane and Katie came, they left, Biddy and Daniel came, Pam and Bob came then Julia, Peter and the children came - 12 for lunch - I made a huge meal in the Wok - in half an hour - proud of that! About 4pm most people drifted off - Bri took Biddy and Daniel to Bath station - Jenny and David arrived (school friends) they stayed till 6 - they left - I collapsed for ten minutes then did washing and ironing! ('cos life goes on and Meg was going off on the Monday morning and Chris needed a shirt for work!).

Eventually went to bed around 10.30 - and kept waking up - remembering all the nice things that had happened and thinking of all the things I have to do before going back to school.

Bri and I thoroughly enjoyed the whole four days - especially getting our friends to meet each other. We had a super time - loved it - apart perhaps when everyone arrived on the Saturday

140

but even that had its fun side.

Monday Meg drove off *(in Ebet's car)* to Sheffield - Bri and Chris went to work and I wrote 30 thank you letters and began my epistles to you! (I've actually written them all within 2 days but am sending them separately for more fun and so I can add any news. (It's now Tuesday in case you're confused!!) (16th August).

Thought you might like to know what our pressies were, so will include a list! We told folk we wanted them, not pressies - but they were so generous. We feel very blessed to have such good friends and family.

Bri's back to work and the sun's out - Meg is returning on Sunday or Monday and I have work to do - boring!! So dear Dad and Mum though you couldn't be with us I hope at least you feel now part of the celebrations - you probably know more than most as to the order of things, you certainly were not forgotten.

Love you lots and thanks again for the super pressie - so sorry that your celebrations *(their anniversary was on 14th August)* were rather spoilt by poor Julia's dad having flu - hope you had fun with Barbara!

All love, God bless

Lizzie XXX

PS. One thing I forgot to tell you about the Orfe - when I first tried to get it out of the pond I used this huge plastic bag - got about a ton of water in, stood up triumphant - then found there was lots of little holes in the side. It looked like a living sculpture water fountain - sure the fish laughed.

Fifteen years later found Liz and Brian celebrating again. This time, of course, it was the Ruby wedding anniversary.

"YOU ARE THE JEWELS IN OUR CROWN"
Speech given by Liz at the Ruby wedding anniversary celebrations

Well, this is a bit good - to quote our dear friend Sam. Thank you so much for making the effort to be with us and making this a very special day.

The themes for today, Brian and I decided, are 'Hearts, Love and Friendship'.

Throughout my life friends have been the most important factor - whether they be In-laws or Out-laws or Others and when I look around here today I think I must be one of the luckiest, most blessed people in the whole world. All I see are friends. Some of you I have known for 50 years and some of you are far too young for me to have known that long. Some of you have travelled miles and some from just next door.

Some of you have come; Bryan and Liz, when I'd have thought you had every excuse not to. It's sad that some folk who we would dearly have loved to see aren't here - either because Australia and America are a bit far - or holiday dates had already been fixed before the invitations went out - or something else had cropped up or very sadly because that person has died and we grieve for the loss of their presence – however you are here and you are all most precious to us, you are all so special that we wanted you to get to know each other, even if just a little bit - hence the photo competition and table quiz - and because you are so special we had the tables named after gems - you are the jewels in our crown.

However, at the risk of seeming prejudiced there is one here who is my best friend.

He is also my husband, the father of our two boys, Andy and Chris, (of whom we are inordinately proud and whom we treasure), and the great love of my life. I know we worry some folk 'cos we apparently argue - "Oh, for goodness sake you two," was heard in exasperated tones just a few months ago - and on one occasion I was taken on one side by a dear friend who was worried about the state of our marriage. I upset him a little, 'cos I giggled.

I came across a really interesting statement the other day in a Margery Allingham book would you believe; Quote "Love isn't a cement, it's a solvent" - or in my words, love is a fusion rather than a joining. Brian and I aren't stuck with each other, we have merged!

We have known each other since I was about eleven, and started going out about forty three years ago.

Twenty years ago Brian had his first of five heart attacks. I can remember very clearly what I was feeling as I drove with Chris and Andy to the hospital.

Strangely enough I was feeling grateful; grateful that we had had 20 special years together. You can imagine how I feel now, after another 20 years together.

Brian is the most amazing, honest, brave, straight-forward, generous, active, practical, hardworking, loving person I know and I love him to bits. I am just so grateful to those doctors and surgeons and nurses who have kept on putting him together for me. That's why we are having a collection for The British Heart Foundation.

We will pass around Brian's Australian hat, and any donation will be gratefully received. We have even got some Gift Aid forms you can fill in if you pay tax and you'd like to.

Also I'll be giving the answers and specially commissioned prizes for the poetry competition and photo competition during coffee.

Finally, Brian and I are so delighted that you are here to celebrate our 40th wedding anniversary with us as we wanted to say our Thank You to you very special people.

During the service held to celebrate this occasion, Liz read this poem by George Herbert.

LOVE
George Herbert

Love bade me welcome, yet my soul drew back,
  Guilty of dust and sin.
But quick-ey'd Love, observing me grow slack
  From my first entrance in,
Drew nearer to me, sweetly questioning
  If I lack'd anything.

"A guest," I answer'd, "worthy to be here";
  Love said, "You shall be he."
"I, the unkind, the ungrateful? ah my dear,
  I cannot look on thee."
Love took my hand and smiling did reply,
  "Who made the eyes but I?"

"Truth, Lord, but I have marr'd them; let my shame
  Go where it doth deserve."
"And know you not," says Love, "who bore the
blame?"
  "My dear, then I will serve."
"You must sit down," says Love, "and taste my
meat."
  So I did sit and eat.

From *The Temple: Sacred Poems And Private Ejaculations* 1633

***

Other writing

Liz was an extremely talented drama teacher and she had her own inimitable and unforgettable style of relating to her teenage students. This developed over time and through experience. It wasn't easy, especially at the beginning…

5Z

The noise from inside the classroom was horrific. 5Z were inside. I had not yet met this class but their reputation was school if not town-wide. At 22 years old and five foot two I did not feel I had the confidence or ability to face 5 let alone 5Z.

I took a deep breath, hoped that my shaking wouldn't be noticed and opened the door.

I've often wondered what an ant must feel like walking through grass - now I knew - not a lad in there appeared under 6ft. 2 inches and the fact that some of them were standing on desks made it worse.

The noise stopped as I got half-way to the front - then whispers and giggles began.

I smiled.

Hullo 5Z I have been so looking forward to meeting you!

THROUGH THE ROOF
(Adventures of a drama teacher)

Some years ago, while teaching in a very large comprehensive school, I was 'given' a class of boys with learning difficulties and emotional problems. They were between 13 and 14 years old - and I don't know about learning difficulties because they ran rings round me the first time we met.

Luckily there were only about fifteen in the class, so when, during our first encounter they spotted a hole in the roof, before you could blink, they had dragged a table and a chair underneath the said hole and gone through it.

I was able to get them down 45 minutes later, just before the bell went!

Obviously a new strategy was needed.

The following week, I arrived a few minutes late to make sure the boys were all there.

Ignoring them, I walked, head down, to the middle of the room, sat down on the floor and began to cry.

The arrogant chatter about what they were planning to do today gradually broke off, to be followed by a lot of rather anxious whispering. A few minutes later the boys, now down to my level, on their knees, crawled across the floor towards me, and a brave soul whispered: "What's the matter, Miss?"

"My name's Simon, and I'm really frightened as I have to fight a dragon and I don't know how to," and I sobbed violently.

A lot of hasty discussion followed, then a big lad stood up and said,

"Don't you worry, Simon, we'll help you. My dad's got a JCB and that will flatten any dragon,"- and we were off.

Over the following weeks the magic of what is

known as 'educational drama' took over. The boys were faced with a giant spider, a robot, a shape-shifting dragon (all me) and all in situations that needed problem-solving skills.

Then I would appear as Simon saying that I had been too frightened and had been hiding and I didn't know what had happened.

The boys would then recount to me what they had done and how they had outwitted all these other characters - all rôle-played by me!

It is a true delight and one of the great joys of this type of drama that children of all ages respond in this way and truly 'suspend disbelief.'

And the purpose of telling this story? Well, often when becoming Simon and handing to the boys the responsibility of the drama action, I'd remember the words of Jesus,

"Unless you become as a little child..." and muse on the fact that by doing so I, and the boys, had had a real fun time and a huge amount had been achieved.

SOMEONE

Someone was coming. He could hear the heavy tread of footsteps on the uncarpeted floor. He froze, his hands clasping tightly the handles on either side of the chest on which he was sitting. Sounds were close now. Panic made him move. Fear had kept him gripped in stillness, now blind panic made him rush for the side door. The twisting narrow staircase seemed to move also as he made a headlong dash down its spirally length.

The door at the bottom was locked. He turned the handle - screamed in frustrated anger, beat hideously on the door with his tiny fists. He turned eventually, his back burying itself in the wood beams of the door and peered up at the advancing figure.

Why there you are Jimmy said a well-loved voice - what game are you playing now.

The five year old looked up at his father and a smile crept across his tear smudged face.

Incidents at home would also inspire Liz to reach for her pen...

OUR GREMLIN

Anyone who knows us well will also know of our Gremlin. He (and for some reason I am convinced it's a he) has been with us since we got here over 38 years ago.

His favourite antics usually concern water or electricity and have been known to make grown workmen tear out their hair, if not actually cry. One, I remember, who said he'd come in the late afternoon to fix something quite simple looked at me most oddly when I told him we had a Gremlin and would he mind coming early in the morning as I was positive that the job would take much longer than he had forecast.

He obviously thought me quite mad but as we were paying the bill he agreed.

He arrived at 8am. He finally left at 8pm and

had to be called back at 9pm as our ceiling was sagging as a result of a leak.

He told me that never had he come across anything like the problems he had encountered and we were welcome to our Gremlin! I had warned him!

One of the weirdest tricks played was when the door between the kitchen and the laundry room locked. Weird, because there is no lock on this door, and particularly annoying as our back door was locked and the keys to the shed (where the tools are kept) are in the laundry room.

Finally a screwdriver was found and the whole handle removed. The door refused to budge. I got so mad that I actually reproved the gremlin out loud – told him he'd had his fun and that enough was enough. On my word of honour the door then opened!

You can perhaps see why I don't scoff at our 'lodger'.

The following story, written by Liz, was published in the parish magazine for Holy Trinity Church, Bradford on Avon, in December 2007.

THE DONKEY'S TALE

I didn't want to go at first. I'm not that young any more. I knew I was going to have to journey somewhere.

All the humans were in a stir about having to be 'registered', whatever that meant. If I was needed it was because I would have to carry something, or someone, a long way. I didn't want to go at all.

The man who came to get me didn't seem too bad. He had a kind voice and patted my neck. I like my neck being patted. He told my master that he had to travel from Nazareth, (that's where I'm stabled), to Bethlehem. That's a long way. He seemed even more anxious than the other men around. I heard him saying that his wife was expecting a baby, and it was due very soon.

'Trouble', I thought. 'Why me?' The wife's name was Mary. She patted my neck too and said she hoped she wouldn't be too much of a burden. Young she was and though it was obvious that her baby was due soon, when I carried her she seemed no weight at all!

The journey was hard. For six days we travelled, and although at first Mary walked alongside me and the man (Joseph was his name, by the way), I had to carry her for the last two days. I knew her baby was due any time soon and I tried to go more quickly. Joseph was very good to me and praised my efforts.

I was so pleased when we reached Bethlehem but Oh! it was so crowded. There were people everywhere, all rushing and pushing. I was so tired and really looking forward to being in a warm stable for a night, but when we got to the inn, Joseph was told he was too late. All the rooms were taken. I wished, then, that I had tried to go even faster and Joseph kept telling the innkeeper that they couldn't have got to Bethlehem any earlier because his wife was about to have a baby. The innkeeper just said he couldn't help that, there just wasn't any room in the inn. Then, do you know what Joseph did? He said could he at least stable me for the night? I was so surprised - to think about me at a time like this!

I think the innkeeper was a bit surprised too, because he was quiet for a minute and then said not only could I be stabled for the night but so could Mary and Joseph.

I was so pleased, for a stable is a wonderfully warm and cosy place.

Well, what a night it was! We had only just got settled into the stable and I'd managed a greeting or two to the other animals (there were cows and horses and mules and even a dog I remember), when Mary had her baby.

We could see the little mite as there was a really bright light shining through the rafters. It was very strange but later we heard that a star above the stable had started to shine really brightly. I never actually saw the star but I certainly saw the light. So bright it was.

You'd have thought all that was excitement enough but we had all just started to settle down again, the baby having been cleaned and laid in the manger, made comfy with straw, and Mary resting and Joseph fussing, when there was the sound of rushing feet and the stable door burst open and standing there were shepherds, all breathing very hard and looking - well I don't know how to describe how they looked - excited and frightened and as if they were expecting something wonderful, and then they behaved as if they were seeing something wonderful!

They came in and bowed before Mary and Joseph and asked to see the boy child (who, by the way, had been called Jesus). They told how they had seen great lights and things they called Angels who had told them not to be afraid as they were being given news of great joy and that a baby had been born in the stable of the inn in Bethlehem. He was to be the saviour of the world.

Soon the stable was filled with all sorts of folk, and the shepherds told their story over and over again. Finally the shepherds left calling out and praising God, and slowly all the other people left too, but only after they all had a peek at the baby.

Nobody laughed at the shepherds or called them names, but many said they, too, had seen strange sights on the hills and, after all, there was the star over the stable!

And I, what did I think? I decided then and there that no matter what happened to me in the future (that's another story which I may tell you some time), I had been present at the most special, wonderful moment in the world's history and what is more it had all happened in the very best place possible - a stable.

***

'MAKE POETRY AND GIVE PLEASURE'
(Quintus Horace Flaccus - Roman Poet)

As well as letters and stories, Liz could produce poems for all occasions, whether to amuse her children or as a way of saying thank you to friends or just for fun. Some poems were simply personal reflections on life.

To end this book, we have included a selection of these.

CHRISTOPHER PAUL
There was a little boy called Christopher Paul
Who wasn't very big and he wasn't very tall
He never did come when his mummy did call
In fact he never did as he was told at all
Round and rubbery like a ball
Full of cheek and even more.

SAM IS A MAN
Sam is a man
Who has a dog
But thinks it is a pig
And so he now surrounds himself
With pictures small and big
Which show the features glorious
Of porcine handsomeness
And style that he appreciates
Of piggy-like finesse

I wonder if the dog likewise
Has also got confused

Or even knows it is a dog
And if it did would choose
To stay a canine creature
Or choose a piggy state
Because it sees in that man Sam
A truly fine soul mate.

THERE WAS A YOUNG PIG

There was a young pig
Called Oscar-de-Wit
Who many considered
A bit of a nit

His airs and his graces
To behold were a hoot
And many just itched
To give him the boot

With trotters extended
He'd sup up his tea
To be aristocratic
He just longed to be

He'd heard of the proverb
About a sow's ear
So decided like silk
His ears must appear

He never went grubbing
For acorns in dirt
In case his fine snout
Got injured or hurt

He pinned up his tail
In curlers at night
So that in the morning
It might twirl just right

He'd read all the books
On manners and taste
And decided his talents
Must not go to waste

He wanted so much
To be prince of all pigdom
But no one wanted him
So he formed his own kingdom

But a court of just one
No matter how refined
Is enough to drive any pig
Out of his mind

So Piggy he lorded
Over wide and empty hall
Just proving the proverb
Of pride before fall

So just you remember
About Piggy's fate
And don't go pretending
You are what you ain't!

WINTER THOUGHTS ON WINTER WOES

Have you ever really wondered
What happens to a sneeze
As it sets off on its journey
With extraordinary ease

It must surely travel forward
Not ever turning back
Until it meets an obstacle
Or impetus does lack

The sufferer who's left behind
Continues on to wheeze
Only stopping momentarily
A handkerchief to seize

Beware the sneeze that is not blocked
For it surely carries sorrow
The nasty germs must soon be stopped
Or you might sneeze tomorrow

DRAMA TEACHING

We have come here to express to you just what
we all have learned
About ourselves, and drama, the way in which
we've turned -
From funny little robots with no minds of our
own
Into thinking, feeling people who strife and
work and hone -
The ideas of a moment into something we can

157

use -

To stretch imagination, give us interesting views.

We have mounted expeditions, crossed ravines and mountains too;

We have starred in main productions, that we really like to do;

We have been out to the theatre, and we're doing that again;

We have worked in groups of twenty, and of four and three and ten;

We have created legends, lived on islands, learned to dance;

We have visited in heaven, learned you've got to take a chance;

We have found that we are capable of many different skills;

We have done away with boredom, learned of truth without the frills;

We have learned it all by doing and then thinking what we've done,

Reflecting on the reason that we've come to talk to you,

We think we're better better people 'cos we care 'bout what we do,

And this then is the reason that we've come to talk to you,

'Cos now you have this option that will help you get through life,

That will help you with the working and the thinking and the strife.

We want to say 'do take it' for drama is the tool,

Amongst the many options it really is the jewel.

TO MUM NETLEY

There was a Mum Netley
Little but bold
Who was worth much more
Than her weight in gold

She's great at all she does
And she does almost all
You should see how she handles
A round wooden ball

We can't wait to see
Our little Mum crowned
When she grinds down the opposition
Into the ground

So good luck Mummy Netley
But win or lose,
You are the mum
We would always choose

So go out there fighting
Go out with a grin
And if wishing can make it
You must surely win

We wish we could be there
And in thought we will be
Wishing our mum on
To fine victory

For Brian's father

THERE ONCE WAS A BEAR

There once was a bear
So big and so gruff
That some thought him rude
And some guessed him tough

He had a deep growl
That rumbled deep down
A really fierce stare
And formidable frown

And yet in his eyes
A deep twinkle there lay
And sometimes a smile
On his lips would play
A mischievous humour
Lay lurking below
The outer stern front
That he put on for show

And many were caught
Into thinking that Ted
Never had funny thoughts
Deep down in his head

And some they were caught
By his acting sly
'Cos he weren't fierce at all
Only every so shy

And his chief joy of all

161

Was to tempt and to tease
To make others gasp
And to giggle and sneeze

An astonishing bear
You will have to agree
With his naughtiness there
For all who could see

And if Teddy dear
You think it is true
That this cuddly bear
Is somewhat like you

Then all I can say
Is it wonder I call
You Teddy Edward
The best loved of all

For Brian's father again
WHERE ARE YOU?
If you're confused, then think of me,
The problems that I face,
Not only just what to write,
But where the heck's your base.
The postmen and the nurses
Could be scratching heads with doubt
As to where to send Ted Netley's post
Now that he's got out.
But - if you are still sitting there
And haven't yet got home
It could be, when you get this
You'll find solace in this po(e)me!

WHAT TO WRITE?
Do you know
I'm sitting here
And wondering what to write?
The crockery is waiting
And the washing's dirty white
The children will
Be rushing in,
All gasping for their tea;
The carpet is knee-deep in dust
The room's not fit to see.
The rain outside
Is pouring down
So the gardening can't be done
(Well - I wouldn't do it anyway,
Not my idea of fun);
So I sit here,

And I sit here,
Wondering what on earth to say
That will tell yer how we loves yer
And I think of you each day;
But it seems to me
The 'Muse' has left
And though I chew my pen
There's nothing I can really do
To bring it back again;
So I thought maybe
I'd tell you
I've been trying with all might
With crossings-out and sighings
To think of what to write.

OUR ALLEY
Our alley is a merry old place
On one side the old, narrow, slender houses
sway up to the sky and on the other side
of the winding paved 'way' are
the gardens where ancient trees do grow
You can hear the sound of babies crying,
birds singing, and crickets clicking
A hop-scotch board is drawn out
with stones on our alley
waiting for the rain to wash it away
A scent of cooking dinners
drifts through open windows.
All sizes of windows
through which you can glimpse
wood panelled walls,
antique china & shining brass.
A merry old place is our alley

OUR THANKS

The rain it poured,
The wind did sound,
Our tennis hut
It left the ground.

But Pete with drive,
And Mick his mate,
With Bob, Les and Roy
Just didn't wait.

They worked with hammer
With nails and saw
Till hut again
Had roof and floor.

So thanks to all
For work and cash
For all your verve
And all your dash.

Our hut is raised our glasses too
We raise in gratitude
To you.

AN APOLOGY

Oh Dear Chris
All bristly and bold
It has often been said
And more often told
That jesting at another's gifts
And seeming most cold

When confronted with beauty
(like your cardboard in fold)
Is jealousy; so guard your ability
Hoard it like gold

When I saw your creation
So smooth in design
I heaved an inward sigh
And wished it was mine.
The curves so sublime
The perpendiculars too
Oh how I wish I could make things
Just like you!

So my old love
Let me make it clear
That my nasty comment,
The lips in a sneer
Were brought from my soul
Where envy did boil
'Cos I bow in admiration
To your art work,
My dear

Please don't bar me from your door
Say I may enter just once more
To gaze in silence
Wondrous awe
At your garage
With the swinging door!

FOR JAN AND IAN

An Eb she went a walking
And she met a Jan one day
A limping on her left leg
And one to other did say
"You must come & have a coffee"
And after some time this they did
Meet & fell a-talking
Oh what a friend Jan became to Eb!

Upon the scene came Ian
And from his lofty bearded height
Beamed upon a little Brian
One cold December night.
We all began to chatter
And got on mighty well
Till that hairy beast called Ian
Taught a card game that was hell!

However we survived this
Despite that 'last card' call
And we even went a dancing
At ye old St. Margaret's Hall,
Other dates we then fixed up
And enjoyed them all with glee
Especially some shocked comments
'bout little Ian and me!!

The kiddies too, they get on fine
And hardly ever fight
Tho' Collette & Herbie cause concern
Oh! What a shocking sight
And with giggles & with chatter

There is nothing ever lacking
So will finish with this last line
Jan & Ian give great <u>Back</u> - ing!!

BIRTHDAY GREETINGS
An instant ode
To two who now
Are reaching years of knowledge
This greeting from
The rest of us
Who've managed through life's college;
For fifty is a mighty sword
To slice through life's adventure,
You're young enough to forward look
And old enough to censor
Those things which would be boring
Or of negative reward
And welcome open handed
Those things to be adored.
We wish you 'Happy Birthday'
And many more great years
And may you both continue
To smile through any fears.
We value you as family,
We value you as friends,
You're very special people
And so this greeting sends
Our warm congratulations
Our wishes full of love
For you dear Jan and Ian
Are really far above
The normal, mundane mortals

Who walk upon the earth
For like the great Colossus
You both have wondrous girth.

PS
Dear both, I couldn't find the original - you
may have it Jan, 'cos
I passed it to you at the dinner table! However
the ending is slightly
different ('cos I couldn't' remember quite what
I put) but it isn't an
insult. Colossus bestrode the world with
magnificence - and that was
what I was trying to say - not about your size.
Thanks for a lovely
evening. Love you lots. Ebet & Brian

TO BARBARA
I thought I'd write you, one more time,
In couplets ending in a rhyme, to let you know
how glad are we
That back home safely now you be.
And if this seems contrived somewhat
With words reversed ---- a jumbled lot
Remember please, with sympathy,
That rhyming couplets hardest be
To write in, making sense the while
Yet somehow keeping flowing style
That pleases ear and mind as well
While managing yourself to tell
We loves yer, and could shout with joy
That you're back home once more with Roy

And that last couplet awful be
Enough to make you wince at me
'Cos now me rhymes got out of hand
I'll have to try and make a stand
To grab the pen and put it down
Before I really make you frown.
I'll say 'goodbye' before I curse
And find I'm doing that in verse!

THE SILLY OWL
There was an owl
Sat in a tree
And watched the world
Go by
The other birds thought him a hoot
And need you wonder why
The other birds
Could sing and call
And make the woodland bright
While all the silly owls did
Was "twit twoo" at night

THE INVINCIBLE
Each separate being
Seeking,
Longing for a new identity,
Searching,
Sometimes unknowingly,
In the morass of
Uniformity,
For their individuality.

For mundane triviality,
Strangles initiative,
Suffocates creativity,
Creating inertia.
The spark of genius
In all individuals
Is smothered in darkness
Of each working day.

But the knowledge of
Seeking,
This awareness of knowledge
Is almost enough,
We can still just say -
Tomorrow
And
Tomorrow
I will find,
I will be,
I can, I shall,
Tomorrow - we'll see.

INNER BEING

There is an inner being,
Thing,
That rebels
Causes
An image to project
Of all that could be made
Of muscles
Bone & tissue
We squash it,

Soak it in ennui,
Neglect it,
Yet it lives.

Fights against forgetfulness
Forces itself
To our consciousness
and Shouts
With intensity
"Come Exist
As I exist, --
and Be.

QUESTIONS
Amidst the blood
Is there confused
Conflict of hope?
Can insight, slightest knowledge
Of love and goodness
Be heard through
The drippings of smashed bodies?
Can one keep life going
While living?
Can compassion
Defeat compulsion?
Is all despair ultimately?
Can the guttering candle cause a conflagration?
Must evil be destroyed
By destruction,
Enemies' weapons
Therefore tainted,
Or is fear

All that must be feared?
Can each day dawn,
Each morning break,
Each minute pass
Without death being the victor,
The beginning of the end and final
Conqueror?
Can the passion of love
Outshine into obscurity
The passion o fanaticism?
Can not the world,
Each individual, throbbing vital
Being of the world
Break the conviction
Of total conviction?
Can we be still,
Fracture the roars of protestation,
The animal cries of
Dictatorship,
Pierce with the quiet
Gentle words
That could engulf, encircle
And pulsate through
Time and space
"But you see…..we care"

THINK 'PINK' ON A BLACK DAY

When 'thinking positive' seems a negative
thing to do -
Think Pink!
When the energy needed to be courageous
seems a waste of effort -

Think Pink!
When nightmares take the place of dreams -
Think Pink!
When other people's acts of kindness grate
upon the soul -
Think Pink!
When future plans are hindered and it's difficult
to plan at all -
Think Pink!
When your mind screams but you're forced to
smile -
Think Pink

Pink is the first lighting of the sky
Flushed with the success of being born.

Pink is neither insipid nor strident;
It has within it the fire of passion
And the blazing white of faith.

Pink has the strength of burning embers
Which can be rekindled with a breath.

Pink is the colour of hope and promise.
Think, therefore, 'Pink' on a black day.

***

CONCLUSION

'MANY WATERS CANNOT QUENCH LOVE, NEITHER CAN THE FLOODS DROWN IT'
(Song of Solomon 8:7)

Liz was no ordinary person. Everything about her, from her glasses to her personality was 'writ large'.

She wasn't merely gifted; she was immensely talented in many different, creative areas. She didn't just know a number of people, she had an extraordinarily large number of close friends, as demonstrated by the enormous response we had to our request for material for this book. She was not only ready to share; she was abundantly generous with her money, her talents and her love. She was not simply a good teacher; she was an outstanding guide and mentor who exercised a profound and lasting influence on her students.

Most of all, she possessed a boundless supply of love and compassion which was freely distributed to all with whom she came in contact.

This is her legacy; and this is why all those whose lives were touched by her, will never forget Elizabeth Netley.

www.ingramcontent.com/pod-product-compliance
Lightning Source LLC
Chambersburg PA
CBHW062106080426
42734CB00012B/2773